HACKETT'S

A REFEREE'S NOTEBOOK!

LAW

HACKETT'S

A REFEREE'S NOTEBOOK!

LAW

KEITH HACKETT

WILLOW BOOKS
Collins
8 Grafton Street, London
1986

Willow Books
William Collins Sons & Co. Ltd
London · Glasgow · Sydney · Auckland
Toronto · Johannesburg

© Keith Hackett 1986

BRITISH LIBRARY CATALOGUING IN PUBLICATION DATA
Hackett, Keith
Hackett's law: a referee's notebook
1. Soccer – Refereeing
I. Title
796.334'3'0924   GV943.9.R43

ISBN 0-00-218076-6

Cartoons by Paul Davies

Diagrams by Studio Briggs

Photoset in Palatino by Cheney & Sons Ltd, Banbury
Printed and bound in Great Britain by
Wm Collins Sons & Co. Ltd, Glasgow

Contents

Acknowledgements

My thanks go first to John Etheridge of Hayters who helped to bring this book to fruition; then to the two main governing bodies of English football, the Football Association and the Football League; to my own guardians the Referees' Association and the Association of Football League Referees and Linesmen; and finally to the Sheffield and Hallamshire County FA, who gave me the early encouragement to become a class one referee.

1
The Cup Final

April Fools Day 1981 looked like being conspicuously short of jokes. I had just refused the Football League's invitation to handle a game between Ipswich Town and Arsenal, a crucial match with both teams challenging at the top of the First Division. I was injured and likely to be out for some time. Referees, like players, must be honest with themselves; if you cannot run, you cannot officiate. Nevertheless, I hate having to turn down matches.

Earlier that Wednesday morning I visited Barry Claxton, the Rotherham United physiotherapist, for ultrasonic treatment on my painful bruised Achilles tendon. I enjoy refereeing and, although not exactly suffering manic depression, I was deeply disappointed at the prospect of a lengthy absence from the middle.

As I stood in the hall and stared through the window, lost in my own frustration, I was jerked from my thoughts by the shrill tone of the telephone. I immediately recognised the voice. Reg Paine, the FA Referees' secretary, was a regular caller, but I will never forget our brief conversation that day.

'What are you doing on May 9?' asked Reg.

Funnily enough, that date was imprinted on my mind, not for the game at Wembley, but because I had promised to present the prizes for an event called the Purdie Cup, a competition held on the outskirts of Sheffield in memory of a player who had died from a kidney complaint.

'I've got a presentation,' I replied.

'Oh,' said Reg. 'Well I've got some good news for you.'

'What's that?'

'You're refereeing the FA Cup Final.'

I was stunned. I could hardly believe what I was hearing. But, yes, it was true. I had actually been chosen for the 1981 Centenary Cup Final between Tottenham Hotspur and Manchester City. Every referee, when he takes the field for his first match on a local park, in his gleaming new kit, thinks 'Wembley – that's the place I'd like to reach.' In real life, it seldom happens, but my dream had become reality.

The telephone trembled in my hands. Here was somebody offering me domestic football's greatest honour and I was lost for words – which is something that rarely happens. I was thirty-six and had been on the Football League list for less than five seasons. I had thought of plenty of referees who might be given the appointment and I most certainly was not among them. I wanted to tell everybody, but had been asked to remain silent until the two linesmen and reserve official had been informed.

I wanted to share this moment with, in particular, other referees. We are a close-knit fellowship and they would have appreciated what it meant to me. Referees spend a lot of time in each other's company, swapping opinions, discussing decisions and providing guidance.

This kaleidoscoped through my mind as I replaced the receiver, walked through the lounge and into the kitchen where Ian Bilson, a refereeing colleague, was having coffee with my wife Lynda. I simply said: 'Great news. That was Reg Paine. I've got the FA Cup Final.'

Pandemonium. Ian ran berserk, jumping up and down, and I punched the air. They were a marvellous few moments. A few doubts crossed my mind when my eldest son Paul pointed out that it was April 1. There are a few jokers in the refereeing fraternity, but surely none could be so cruel. Then I had a telephone call from Radio Hallam, the local independent station in Sheffield, who had heard the news, and my delight quickly became public.

For the next five weeks, the phone rang incessantly with well-wishers and people asking me for interviews, photographs and tickets. I believe the appointment should be shared and the man in the middle at Wembley is representing all the referees in the country, so I used the demands on my time by Press and public to give people an insight into the job and a preview of what could be expected from me during the game. My message was: 'I won't change my style for Wembley. I'm a referee who likes to keep the game flowing and will treat the Final in exactly the same way as any other match.'

I took the opportunity to explain certain facets of refereeing, like why I did not always accept a linesman's flag for offside. Thousands of people might be screaming at the linesman to place his flag somewhere less polite than in the air, while the rest want the referee to open his eyes because he is missing an offside. Other people could not understand why a Football League referee can be at Anfield, Arsenal or Old Trafford one week and Concord Park, Sheffield, the next. Another popular question was, if I was so surprised at getting the appointment, did I ever question my ability to do the job? I stressed that, for about twenty years, I had been refereeing 100 matches a season. That is a lot of experience. Anyway, that was the single most thrilling aspect of the appointment. The Football Association were putting their faith in me to handle their premier occasion; they clearly considered I could do the job, which increased my confidence, a quality vital to all referees.

I was also anxious to present the correct impression. It was essential to remain calm, yet avoid sounding arrogant or indifferent, when being interviewed, so I happily handled all the interviews and telephone calls, although I must confess the photographers occasionally became a nuisance. I dislike posing and one day three cameramen arrived on my doorstep wanting me to stand on the roof of my car, hang from the ceiling and perform a variety of other stunts that I just was not prepared to do.

At no time did I suffer from nerves, but there was one nagging anxiety. While all the ballyhoo was going on, I was still having daily treatment on

my ankle and performing body exercises to stay fit. I had to stay off the injury as much as possible, but participated in a British Steel five-a-side competition to keep my mind alert. Fives are as good for referees as for players because the nature of the game requires a series of rapid decisions. I decided to risk the injury in an effort to stay mentally alive.

I made up my mind that, if I was not fully fit, I would withdraw from the Final. This was a genuine fear. Fortunately, I had great confidence in Barry Claxton, who assured me I would be fit in time. Although not a serious injury, just bruising really, it was painful and needed plenty of attention. Barry gave me a special strapping for the match, just in case. Looking back, I now appreciate it was psychological more than anything. I did use the strapping, but I didn't really need it. Barry had done a marvellous job.

The fear, the dread, that I might have to pull out of the Final had disappeared, though, when Lynda and I drove south on the Friday before the game. We arrived at White's Hotel, in London's Bayswater Road, at about three o'clock and, after unpacking, I was keen to meet my colleagues as soon as possible. A referee and his linesmen should attempt to create a rapport before any match and the axiom has never been more important than before the FA Cup Final.

I already knew Dave Hutchinson, the senior linesman, and had seen him referee, while Alan Jones had run the line for me before. John Penrose, the fourth official, to be used if one of us dropped out at the last moment, completed an encouragingly compatible quartet.

That evening I attended the traditional eve-of-Final dinner organised by the London Society of Association Referees. It provided an opportunity to meet referees from all over the world and I was presented with a plaque. The room was dimmed and the spotlight picked out Dave, Alan, John and myself as we entered the Camden Town Hall. For the first time, I suddenly realised quite how important being asked to handle the Cup Final was to all referees. I spotted referees I had looked up to for years, world-renowned officials such as Jim Finney, Ken Aston and Ken Burns. Tonight they were there in my honour.

Ken Burns said some kind words about me and, following a highly relaxed evening, I returned to my hotel with something approaching writers' cramp after signing countless menus and programmes in the time-honoured fashion. I slept well that night, rose early the following morning for breakfast with the other officials and went for a walk in the park. I was ready.

The newspapers were even more full of the Final than usual, because this was the Centenary match. I read as many of the papers as I could in an effort to catch the atmosphere. I had officiated at Wembley twice previously. As senior linesman for the 1979 FA Cup Final in which Arsenal beat Manchester United 3-2 in those dramatic dying minutes, I had closely monitored how referee Ron Challis conducted himself, before, during and after the game. I learnt a lot. My other game at Wembley was a youth clubs' final with Clive White in charge.

We visited the FA headquarters in nearby Lancaster Gate for a glance behind the scenes and then our two chauffeur-driven Daimlers arrived. The luxury drive, apart from being part of the prestige and history of the Wembley Final, provided an essential aspect of the build-up. We were being looked after, almost wet-nursed, and clearly nothing was too much trouble. We reached the outskirts of Wembley and the spectators were already beginning to arrive.

I remember in 1979, we were in the car when this huge individual, bedecked in red and white, peered in, his nose pressed against the window. He shouted, 'Who the hell are you? It's rich buggers like you that get tickets – people that know nowt about football.' His antics gave us a laugh, and again we had a relaxed journey to the twin towers.

Spectators, sporting blue and white hairstyles, scarves, banners, hats and flags, were shouting good-natured comments such as, 'Give us a penalty, ref!' and 'Have a good game!' and in the bowels of the stadium, where security was tight, people were saying things like, 'Suppose we'd better let you in.' The quiet as we entered the stadium was unbelievable – a carnival outside, but as silent as a morgue inside. Arriving early was all part of the preparation. Had we walked in at two o'clock, the atmosphere would have hit us like there was no tomorrow. As it was, we became acclimatised as the crowd grew.

I had used the dressing room before, but was still surprised at how drab and dank it was. You expect more from your national stadium. It is so bare that, at first, you think it leads somewhere else. It is clinical – bare walls, cold floor with the drone of the air-extractor almost lamenting its sad surroundings. You are totally cut off from the crowd, apart from an ancient tannoy on the wall struggling to keep you in touch with the outside world. It served to accentuate the atmosphere when I walked from the chilly confines of the dressing room to the sunlit pitch.

The FA provided a bag containing all the accessories we could possibly require – spare balls, pumps, flags and so on – and, after selecting a couple of balls, we walked out onto the pitch. The photographers clicked into action and, once they let us go, we did a fifteen-minute interview with Pete Murray, who was broadcasting his *Open House* programme direct from the pitch. We checked the nets and the surface looked in excellent condition.

We were heading back into the tunnel to join our wives for a meal when, amid a sudden burst of activity, we were held back by a security cordon. A Jaguar pulled up and out climbed Margaret Thatcher, the Prime Minister. We were introduced and had a brief chat with her and husband Denis who, as a former Rugby referee, took an immediate interest. Mrs Thatcher also brought our wives into the conversation and admitted she had genned up on the teams and the match itself by reading the papers on her journey down from Scotland that morning. She was trying to give us encouragement and we appreciated that.

After a light lunch, we went out onto the gallery between the twin towers to watch people coming up Wembley Way. Standing there, alone with my thoughts, I started thinking. I was looking forward to receiving my medal yet, at the same time, I wanted to have earned it. Years later, I would then be able to think, 'The 1981 Cup Final was a terrific match – and I played my part in it.' Then I said to myself, 'I'm going to have to be careful I don't drop a clanger here today.' The occasion was finally getting to me.

An awareness of the magnitude of my duty, rather than self-doubt, occupied my mind. I returned to the dressing room and went out onto the pitch again, attempting to familiarise myself with the environment. The anticipation and excitement grew as the crowd swelled.

By now, I was anxious to get changed. I had a totally new outfit – right down to the boots – supplied by the Referees' Association and it still hangs in my wardrobe as a permanent reminder of the day. Indeed, I have kept all my Wembley souvenirs, including a little FA booklet, explaining the pre-match procedure. With the ceremony being transmitted to a worldwide television audience of hundreds of millions, everything had to be just right.

We went into the teams' dressing rooms, trying to create an impression of composure. I checked the players' studs and took the match ball with me, throwing it to the goalkeepers – Joe Corrigan and Milija Aleksic – to give them an opportunity to handle it and relieve their tension.

The fat half of Little and Large was in the City dressing room, supposedly there to help the players relax, but he looked more nervous than anyone. We broke the ice by checking the soles of his shoes, which raised a laugh, but, with both dressing rooms a hive of activity, I suspected the managers wanted us in and out as quickly as possible.

We returned to our dressing room and, for the next fifteen minutes, I ran through my pre-match instructions, ensuring the two linesmen understood exactly what I wanted from them and were aware of what I was likely to do in certain situations. Twenty minutes before the kick-off, a head popped round the door and we were on our way. Into the tunnel, where the teams, standing in parallel lines, were throwing balls about, chatting away and patently itching to get on with it.

The light at the end of the tunnel approached and the strains of *Abide With Me* touched me deeply. I was nervous now, and my mind was flashing back to my early days in refereeing and to the people who had helped me reach this moment, but I felt marvellous. The noise was deafening, I could see the atmosphere lifting the players, yet I still wanted at least to appear calm.

It is a fair walk from the tunnel entrance to the front of the Royal Box. Over sand, across the greyhound and speedway tracks, all the time trying to watch your feet and the multitude of television cables snaking across the pitch. With these moments being beamed all over the world, I did not want to fall flat on my face! The officials were last in line as the Queen Mother and the other VIPs in the group chatted with the players and wished us all a good match.

The captains, Steve Perryman and Paul Power, were summoned by the first blow of the whistle and they exchanged pennants and tossed. The game fairly flew and I realised that, during the first twenty minutes, I had to make some allowances for nerves and permit things to settle. The game was full of contrasts. The hard tackling of players such as City's Gerry Gow, whom I kept a particular eye on in the opening exchanges, and the silken skills of Ossie Ardiles and the like. One clash illustrates the fierceness of the play, yet the sensible attitude adopted by the players.

I played advantage after Garth Crooks had hit Tommy Hutchison very hard. Hutchison went away with the ball and Crooks hammered into him again. With Crooks himself finishing prostrate and the City players standing over him, it looked as though they would hit each other. I ran in, shouted at Crooks, 'You stay on the floor!' and literally pushed Hutchison away to try to prevent a flare-up. It had the desired effect, although my methods were not necessarily out of the referees' manual. It shows, however, that a ref must improvise and think quickly in the heat of a game.

I saw from the reactions of the players that they were accepting my keenness to play advantage. Concentrating so hard on the game, my sole awareness of the fans was their noise. A continuous drone, just 'oohs' and 'aahs', but no distinctive songs or chants registered. I remember both goals in the first game. Hutchison put City ahead with a thumping header and then suffered the agony of an own goal near the end. But the substitution of Tottenham's Ricky Villa, a wretched sight as he walked dejectedly in a semi-circle away from the bench area where manager Keith Burkinshaw, the catalyst of his misery, sat impassively, was my most poignant memory of the match itself.

Psychologically, after eighty minutes, I felt fine. I looked at my watch and thought, 'Keith, this is going into extra time. Conserve a little bit.' So, when I blew the final whistle, I was mentally prepared. Some of the players, though, were not. They looked shattered and could hardly believe they had another half-an-hour to go. If somebody went down with cramp during extra time, it would give all the others an excuse to stop. They were all feeling tired, yet nobody wanted to be the first.

Suddenly I had one injury, then another and I remember thinking, 'Hey, this is breaking the continuity of the game.' I decided to keep play going although, at one stage, they were dropping like ninepins. I was not disappointed that the match remained undecided. It had been an enjoyable spectacle for the fans, and I was happy with my own performance. Players congratulated me, a gesture always appreciated by referees.

As I climbed to the Royal Box, I suddenly thought, 'I wonder if I'm going to get the replay?' This was one eventuality not covered. Then the Queen Mother shook my hand warmly, but there was no medal. I knew then that I would be back on Thursday and my face broke into an unashamed smile. I would be the first man to referee two FA Cup Finals at Wembley.

So it was back to work as usual and the start of preparations for the second game. I forfeited my new boots for an old pair, because I had a large blister on one foot, but the Achilles injury was no trouble. We went through the same procedure, and I made a point of telling my linesmen, 'It's only half-time for us. We must do it again – and as well.'

One newspaper had suggested that I should have sent Gow off in the first match. I was rankled – not by the personal criticism, but by the implication that Gow had been dirty and done something that he had not. Gow was hard, but responded to my refereeing. He was there to stop the likes of Hoddle, Ardiles and Villa controlling the game in midfield and from the start of the second match, he started going in very hard on Ardiles again. I pulled him to one side and said, 'I hope you haven't been reading the papers, because they'll all be screaming you should be off by now.' I remember shouting – so forcefully that it came out clearly on the video recording of the game – 'Gerry, Gerry, just calm down.'

Again the atmosphere was daunting, but the players were more relaxed. One could never become blasé about the reception as the players emerge from the tunnel and I have seen established internationals, even those who had played at Wembley before, staggered by the crescendo of sound.

Villa put Spurs ahead and Steve Mackenzie equalised for City with a spectacular volley. Then I awarded a penalty from which City took the lead through Kevin Reeves. Paul Miller and Chris Hughton combined to bring down Dave Bennett and I had no doubts about awarding the kick. Unfortunately, the penalty prompted the game to become over-zealous. A contest that was fierce, but never dirty, became too physical. For the first time my authority was being questioned and I had to caution players to regain control. I took five names in a short spell, mainly for petty things, like Steve Archibald disputing a corner. He was annoyed and showed it. I said, 'Keep quiet and get on with the game.' But he said something further, so he went in the book.

After ten minutes of nonsense, the game settled down again. Crooks equalised at 2-2, but I was delighted there was no need for a penalty shoot-out. Obviously, we had made contingency plans, earmarking a goal and rehearsing the routine, but a football match – especially one as important as the Cup Final – should be decided by eleven players against eleven. Anything else would have been devaluing.

Fortunately, penalties were not needed because the result was settled by that quite unbelievable goal by Villa. At one stage I thought he would be brought crashing to the ground, but he dribbled past a couple of players, then another, then another and slipped the ball past Joe Corrigan. I was pleased that I had not blown for a foul. Villa turned and ran for his governors' seat – towards Keith Burkinshaw, the man who had substituted him just five days earlier.

The end of the match brought an inherent sadness. It showed on the faces of the players who had run themselves close to exhaustion over two matches and finished with nothing. But nobody lost on that game. A marvellous match, and I was proud to have been part of it.

John Bond, the City manager, made a special point of walking across and congratulating the linesmen and me on our performances. He must have been desperately disappointed and I cherished his kind words. Keith Burkinshaw did likewise, as did the players, who kept knocking on our dressing room door to offer their thanks and best wishes en route to the after-match interviews.

It had been the highlight of my career. There were several landmarks associated with the match and they all served to make it even more precious. Centenary FA Cup Final, first man to referee two finals at

Wembley, first penalty to be awarded for nineteen years – setting the right type of precedents, although never for the sake of it, is always rewarding.

When a referee looks back, Wembley is often viewed as the ideal backdrop to end his career. Yet I was only thirty-six. My question was, 'What's next?' I had followed some great referees on that walk up the Wembley tunnel. So what did they do? Jack Taylor went on to referee the World Cup Final. He must have set that as his target. So did I.

2

Early Days

As I descended from the Royal Box, proudly clutching my medal, my mind drifted back to my early days in Sheffield. To my idolisation of Derek Dooley, to the time my uncle played football on his wedding day, to the hill at Cadman Road and to the literally hundreds of matches I refereed which gave me the experience I still call upon today. A long way from a crowd of 100,000 at Wembley, but I knew this great day would never have happened without that essential education.

The game was a love – near to obsession – with what seemed the entire male population in and around Sheffield, and Derek Dooley was the Messiah. My father took me to Hillsborough to watch Sheffield Wednesday and, like thousands of others, Dooley was the man I went to see. We stood in the Lepings Lane End – the ground has changed considerably since then – and Dooley seemed to score in every game. He had pace, skill and the inherent knack of being ideally positioned to strike at goal. Even as a referee, I have a high regard for players with quality and, as a youngster before I even considered taking up the whistle, this man stood out.

One of the greatest thrills in the early part of my refereeing career was being asked to handle the Derek Dooley All Stars charity matches. I was actually officiating at a match involving a team brought together by my idol. Players from Sheffield Wednesday and United and Rotherham would regularly turn out and I was encountering players of the calibre of Peter Swan, Len Badger, Jim McAnearney and Johnny Quinn. I began to appreciate how these professionals used their skill to advantage and it helped to improve my performance. A player, having been fouled, might retain possession and an advantage could be played. It taught me to adopt a type of delayed decision procedure.

The first time I encountered Derek was when he was coaching Birley Amateurs in one of the local Sheffield leagues. He became extremely involved in the matches, shouting advice and instructions from the touchline. He brought the same swashbuckling enthusiasm to watching others play as he had when playing at centre-forward.

Derek Dooley played for Wednesday and subsequently worked for both Wednesday and Sheffield United as manager and administrator. He scored forty-six goals in thirty league matches for Wednesday in the 1951-52 season. Then tragedy. In February 1953, he fractured his leg during a game, gangrene set in, and eventually amputation was necessary to save his life. His career ended in its prime and the whole of Sheffield shed a tear.

While watching Wednesday, I also took part in one of the first pitch invasions seen in this country, although there was nothing I could do to prevent it! Wednesday had just won the match that secured the club's promotion from the Second to the First Division in season 1955-56. The crowd surged forward and lifted me over the fence out onto the field. It sticks vividly in my mind because, at that time, it was forbidden to run on to the pitch and I had never seen it happen before. Now it is more common practice.

If Dooley provided the inspiration in forging my love of soccer, I certainly received plenty of encouragement from my family. My brother John was a keen player and my uncle, Mal Bingley, a tremendous centre-half with a team called Algoma Sports. When I was twelve, uncle Mal was due to be married to Irene. The trouble was that the wedding coincided with an important cup match Algoma were playing. So Mal, doubtless thinking he must get his priorities right, brought the wedding service forward to eleven o'clock in the morning, allowing him time to leave immediately afterwards and play in the game.

The match was played in particularly muddy conditions and Mal, not unnaturally, wanted to be reasonably clean for the reception, which had been delayed until he returned in the evening. There were no showers, and I vividly remember Mal attempting to wash himself with Jusoda, a popular orange drink at the time. If only the people at the reception had known what his legs looked like beneath his trousers!

I would go with Mal to most of Algoma's matches. One game was at Wadsley Common, a ground out in the sticks miles from anywhere, and, as it was towards the end of the season, the team discovered they were a player short. They asked me to make up the numbers. I was only a kid and had no kit, but I went out and scored a goal. I have rarely been happier.

My regular team, though, was Broomhill Sports. I was captain and full back and, as we were having problems with discipline on the field, the secretary decided that one player should sit a referee's examination, enabling him to pass on the laws of the game to his colleagues. I was selected.

I spent six enjoyable evenings at the Sheffield and Hallamshire County Football Association headquarters in Sheffield, where Syd Robinson and Tom Rabey, two well-known local referees, ran through the laws and attempted to pass on their experience of how to deal with problems on the pitch. At the end of the course, I sat an oral exam in which I was questioned by Jim Bennison, then a linesman on the Football League and since secretary of both Doncaster Rovers and Rotherham United.

Apparently, I supplied satisfactory answers, because Jim informed me that I was now qualified as a class three referee. I left the examination with not the slightest intention of refereeing regularly, but merely pleased that I had passed and was now able to help eliminate some of the problems Broomhill Sports were suffering. But all that was soon to change . . .

A few weeks after passing my class three examination, I received a telephone call from the local county FA asking me to referee a match. As we had no game on that Satuday, I accepted. A couple of days before my debut in black, I suddenly realised that I had no kit. My father frequented a pub in Sheffield called the Parkwood Hotel and one of his drinking friends was a class one referee. This man, perhaps appropriately called Bill Shirt, lent me a uniform, so at least I looked the part.

The match was at Cadman Road playing fields between Sheffield United Juniors and Hillsborough Boys Club. I suddenly appreciated for the first time the difference between being a player and a referee. A player has ten colleagues, with whom he can laugh, joke and chat. A referee is on his own. I felt a very lonely person.

There are two pitches at Cadman Road and they are on a huge slope, like so many grounds in the North of England. As a full-back, it had been necessary to exert myself on a few runs but generally I'd been able to pace myself. I soon discovered that a referee rarely stops running during a match and I felt totally exhausted at the end.

However, I was reasonably pleased with the way the match had gone. The players seemed to enjoy themselves and I was allowing the game to flow as much as possible, blowing only when I felt it necessary to maintain control. As I was walking off the field, Len Swallow, who ran Sheffield United Juniors and whose son Ray was then a Football League official, came up and congratulated me on my performance and asked my name. I mentioned that it had been my first game. 'Stick at it, son,' he said, 'you've got the right temperament and attitude for a ref.' That type of compliment provided enormous encouragement and confidence, which is a crucial facet of refereeing.

About a month afterwards, I controlled my second match and decided to join the Sheffield and District Referees' Association. One evening I went along to the Grand Hotel in Sheffield and listened, quite transfixed, to Ken Aston speak. Ken was already a top referee and later, of course, officiated in the 1962 World Cup Finals in Chile. He was the man who, in his capacity as a FIFA referees' instructor and organiser of officials in the World Cup, walked on to the Wembley pitch during the World Cup in 1966 and persuaded Rattin to return to the dressing room after the Argentinian captain had refused to leave the field when sent off against England.

Ken seemed to have been everywhere and done everything. I was fascinated and made to feel very welcome, although the only people I recognised were one or two from my training course. It was clear referees were like a band of brothers; friendly, knowledgeable and with the good of football their priority.

It was season 1960-61 and I decided to take up refereeing on a regular basis. The winter was severe and I was constantly postponing matches because of the frost and icy conditions, then dashing to the telephone and trying to get an alternative appointment. Occasionally, I would be asked to run the line in the County Senior League and, initially, I felt a bit of a mug carrying a flag, not really sure what to do with it. It did, however, teach me another aspect of the game.

Soon, while still a teenager, I was refereeing more than 100 matches a season, at 7s 6d or ten bob a time. At the start and end of the season, I might handle games three or four nights on the trot and throughout, I would do one on Saturdays and perhaps two each on Sunday. Often I would arrive home with my kit drenched or covered in mud and my wife would have to wash, dry and press it in readiness for the game the next day. The experience I gained in those matches forms the backbone of my refereeing even today. The key to handling matches smoothly is the management of people – anybody can learn the written word – and the best way to learn that is on the pitch itself.

A lot of those games – especially on Sunday mornings – were fierce battles and the referees were hard-pushed to maintain control. Once, I was handling a match at Norton Woodseats, a ground that has a stand and its own special atmosphere. As there were no linesmen, I had to spend much of the game patrolling the line in an effort to spot offsides. There were a few potential flashpoints, which I managed to avoid, and the game was going well.

Then I noticed George McCabe, a FIFA referee who had officiated in the 1966 World Cup a few months earlier, standing on the touchline. I was delighted to be having a good game in front of a colleague I greatly admired. After the match, George knocked on my dressing room door and congratulated me on my performance, adding, 'One word of advice, son. When the ball is in the air, don't follow it. Look at the players. Your job is to keep an eye on them on the ground.' Nowadays, I still occasionally get caught in that bad habit and must tell myself, 'Hey, remember what George McCabe told you.' He was right, of course, because watching the players allows the referee to see any offences that occur before the ball arrives, but it's surprising how many referees still fall into that trap.

The next week, just seven days before I married Lynda, who was decorating our terraced house in Sheffield, I bought a copy of the 'Green

'Un', which is the Saturday evening classified edition of the *Sheffield Star*. George McCabe wrote a regular column, in which he discussed a wide range of refereeing subjects. I was an avid reader. This particular week, though, he wrote, 'Has anyone heard of Keith Hackett? Because if you haven't, you soon will.'

I could have received few more welcome wedding presents – in a footballing sense, at any rate – than this compliment from such a highly-respected official. He had offered me advice after the match. Constructive criticism of a colleague's performance is important. Sharing your experiences allows you to learn quickly.

I am a great believer in the value of the Referees' Association, and I think the FA excelled itself with the appointment of Ken Ridden as national training officer for referees. Since Ken's appointment, there has been an enormous increase in the emphasis on improving referees' and linesmens' skills. Experienced referees are being taught how to use audio-visual equipment and the art of lecturing, so we can pass on our knowledge and experiences to others.

I attended a course at Walsall College. Also present were a number of other Football League referees, officials from non-League soccer and even some from abroad. I could not have had a more rewarding week. A company would spend hundreds of pounds sending prospective managers on a similar business course. We refreshed on the laws and learnt the art of lecturing. So, hopefully, I am now able to address Referees' Association meetings more effectively. That is something I enjoy doing and I have always maintained that it is essential for officials to pass on their experiences to the next generation.

So, if you wish to take up the whistle or flag, you should contact your local county FA or the FA in London. Once you have passed your initial referees' examination, my advice would be to join the Referees' Association. There is great friendship and affinity among referees and, with thousands of members up and down the country, I'm convinced you will learn a lot quickly.

Another incident that increased my self-belief occurred when Ray Walsh, a well-known local referee, rang me one Thursday evening saying he was unable to handle his game on Saturday and asking me to take over. Ray was an NSPCC inspector and had been called to a case. A huge man, both in height and width, similar in build to the enormous Russian linesman in the 1966 World Cup, Ray was a strict disciplinarian. I agreed to referee the match, and indeed felt quite honoured to take a game from Ray, especially as it was a departmental semi-final.

The match was on the Osborne Tools ground and, midway through the first half, Ray appeared on the touchline. As soon as the ball went out of play, I invited Ray to take over, to which he replied, 'No, Keith, you carry on. You're having a good game. Keep it up.' I glowed with pride.

Penistone became a favourite ground of mine. The first time I went there was to run the line at a match involving Penistone Church. I arrived at twelve noon for a three o'clock kick-off and, as the club could not secure the services of another referee, I was asked to handle a match that began at one o'clock. With two matches in one afternoon, I was totally shattered.

A marvellous old character named Arthur Lee, who received the British Empire Medal, *was* Penistone Church. He organised the teas, washed the kit and marked the lines. Arthur asked me to officiate in the Purdie Cup matches, a series of charity games between local amateur clubs that took place immediately after the FA Cup Final every year. They honoured the memory of an ex-Penistone Church player and I seldom missed the games. Except, of course, on 9 May 1981.

Perhaps my first match before a substantial crowd was the Sunday League Cup Final at Bawtry Road. I had linesmen and all the trimmings. There must have been two or three thousand spectators, including the Lord Mayor, who presented me with a plaque.

I achieved my ambition of moving from a class three referee through to class two and, ultimately, to class one. Referees were evaluated by marks awarded by club secretaries. If, at the end of each season, a referee's marks were consistently high – an average of seven plus – he was considered for promotion to the next class.

I was still a regular visitor to Hillsborough, when my refereeing commitments permitted, although by now I observed the matches from a different stance from the days when Derek Dooley was the hero. I used to study the referee's actions as much as the players. I would recommend that any referee keeps a close eye on the official when they watch a game. How he is controlling the match, where he is running, how he gives his signals and how he looks towards his linesmen.

Fitness was something I strove for. When I was beginning my career as a referee, I lived at Parkwood Springs, near the top of a hill, and when I arrived home from work, I would put on my tracksuit and run for around five miles up and down the slopes each evening. It is crucial that a referee is fit and able to maintain his pace for ninety minutes – two hours if a cup match goes to extra time.

When I was in my early teens, I also did some race walking. Although not actually taking part in competitive events, I trained regularly with

Sheffield United Harriers walking team. One night a week I did a five- or six-mile walk at a fast pace and one of between fifteen and twenty miles at a reduced speed on Sundays. At the same time as gaining height, the walking helped me to lose weight rapidly. I had been quite plump.

Speed, though, is as important as stamina. I visited a local football pitch and, apart from lapping it to increase my endurance, I would sprint the length and width, running forwards, backwards and sideways. This forms part of the basic structure for referee training.

Mental alertness is another essential quality. Probably the best way to prepare for the season is by refereeing five-a-side matches. The pace is quick and the referee is required to make a lot of instant decisions. Appearance is also important. A scruffy referee neither commands respect nor inspires confidence. The black uniform should be clean and ironed and boots polished, even to the extent that any white markings should remain white.

When I received my class one certificate, I was promoted to running the line in the Yorkshire League. I thought it was the real McCoy! Everybody was properly kitted out and there were newspaper reports on the matches. I saw several familiar faces of players I was refereeing in Sunday matches.

After three seasons as a linesman in the Yorkshire League, I was elevated to the middle, thanks largely to an unusual incident in a match at Kiverton Park. A man called Peter Spacey, a real football enthusiast but a most vociferous and critical observer, was club secretary at Kiverton Park. Once, he went into the dressing room before a match and told the referee: 'Aye, I see we've got to put up with thee again. I hope thee performs a bit better than last time, because I thought thee had a terrible match. I hope be heck thee earns thy money.'

Peter Spacey was in his usual place close to the touchline, ranting and raving, when J.D. Thorpe, who was refereeing the match, suddenly fell flat on his back. He had been knocked unconscious by a player's flying elbow. He was taken from the pitch on a stretcher and, suddenly, the whistle in my pocket was in use. I took over as referee.

I re-started the match but, for about five minutes, nobody took the slightest bit of notice. I kept blowing the whistle and the players simply continued playing. I was becoming a little concerned, so I blew the whistle as hard as I could and called the two captains together and said, 'Hey, fellows, I am now the man in charge and you'd better start taking notice.' Afterwards, the game went well and I suppose it illustrated that I was capable of refereeing a match at that level.

From a referee in the Yorkshire League, I was appointed to the line in the Northern Premier League on its inauguration in 1968. The difference was amazing. The pace and ferocity with which the matches were played was something I had not previously experienced. A suspect decision, that might have been overlooked as an unfortunate aberration in the Yorkshire League, was simply not tolerated in the NPL. The players were playing for money. I was often making trips over the Pennines to Lancashire, involving me virtually for the whole of each Saturday. Macclesfield, Altrincham, Scarborough, Boston, Worksop, Gateshead and South Shields were all regular venues. I was just one echelon away from the Football League.

Disciplinary proceedings formed – and still do form – a substantial part of my refereeing duties. In my early days, I was particularly anxious that any reports I submitted to the county FA were presented in a well-written manner. I usually drafted out my report on a Sunday evening and took it to work on Monday, when two of my fellow draughtsmen at Mellowes Metal Windows, where I worked at the time, would help me before it was typed. Tony Kennedy, another referee, and Mac Shaw, an ardent Sheffield Wednesday supporter, were always willing to offer assistance and between us we normally produced a comprehensive and literate report.

The fun really started, though, when I had sent off a player for using foul and abusive language. The rules stipulated that the referee, in his report, must state clearly the actual words spoken or shouted by the offender. The typist in the office used to peer accusingly over the top of her typewriter whenever she came to the words. We had quite a few laughs.

I would then send my report to the Sheffield and Hallamshire County FA. When relevant, I would write 'foul and abusive language – not to be opened by female staff' on the outer envelope and place my report inside a second envelope. I later discovered that the lady secretaries at the County FA offices generally looked for and opened these letters first when the post arrived. They were curious to see if there were any ruder words than in the past. It must have increased their vocabulary, if nothing else. One reason why referees, despite what some people might think, do not enjoy cautioning or dismissing players is that they are required to explain the reasons in their report, which means additional writing.

The disciplinary hearings themselves were highly formal affairs in which players were given every opportunity to present their case, state their defence and produce witnesses. The committee members were skilful interrogators, attempting not to catch out a player, but merely to discover the facts.

The county FA secretary for many years was Ernest Kangley, whose renown as an administrator extended far beyond Sheffield. He would sometimes call me into his office, but my fears of censure were quickly allayed and I was summoned, usually to receive shrewd advice. One of the few times he actually criticised me was when he telephoned to tell me, quite rightly, not to use the word 'booked' in my reports. This was terminology invented by the Press, he said. The correct term was 'cautioned'. Even today, when I am typing out my report and write, 'I cautioned this player,' I often think of that telephone conversation.

I had been promoted to the referees' panel of the NPL after three seasons as linesman. During my time in the middle, I was appointed to officiate in a number of their top games, including the Northern Premier

League versus Southern Premier League fixture and the NPL's knockout cup final, second leg, between Runcorn and Stafford in 1974-75.

I was appointed to the Football League's linesmens' list in 1972-73, while still handling matches in the Northern Premier. During my final season in non-League football, I received a letter from the NPL management committee. It arrived in early November 1976, at a time when I had handled only five matches so far that season, but had sent off and cautioned a number of players. The letter said that my marks from the clubs had been poor and that, if they did not improve, I would be removed from the NPL referees' list at the end of the season. This seemed ridiculous, because I was due to come off anyway – to become a Football League referee. This was the second such letter I had received from the NPL management committee. I was somewhat mystified by their attitude, because the marks and comments I was receiving from the Football League assessors – men judging whether I had the qualities necessary to officiate at the highest club level – were very complimentary. It just proves that all young referees must be prepared to accept criticism, grit their teeth and make some people eat their words.

Then an ambition I had cherished since I first took up the whistle as a schoolboy in 1960 was fulfilled. After one season on the supplementary list, I was appointed a Football League referee in 1976.

3

Beer and Sweat
at Concord Park

The Football League is usually regarded as having the greatest depth of talent of any domestic league in the world and here I was, at the age of thirty, taking charge of the best players in the business. Every League match every season presents its own kind of problems and pressures. A crowd of thousands acting as jury on the accuracy of an individual's split-second decision; television and action replays; teams challenging for success or struggling to survive; the incentive of money. Each adds to the excitement of being a Football League referee, but they are quite different problems from those encountered by all referees when they begin their career in minor football.

For a start, nearly all of the ninety-two Football League grounds has a separate dressing room for the referee and linesmen. When I first took up the whistle in Sheffield, I was not always so fortunate. Once I was appointed to a match in the Penistone and District League. I hired a Ford Anglia car for the weekend and drove to the ground near Oxspring. When I arrived I could see nowhere to change, for which the club official apologised, and was advised to change in my car. This was not unusual. Indeed sometimes I had to change, quite literally, behind the bushes.

The match was a local derby and passions were roused. I cautioned three or four players in a fiercely competitive opening ten minutes and eventually the players settled down. After the match, as I was struggling to get my trousers on in the car, the same official thanked me for the way I had handled the match. 'Much better than the chap we had last week,' he said. 'His bad decisions made the players so angry, that they set fire to the referee's hut with him in it!'

The presence of a dressing room on the ground, though, was not always a guarantee of palatial changing facilities. Take Concord Park, for

example. There are around twenty pitches on a huge slope and, before a sports centre was built, all the players and officials changed in a wooden hut with no light. Once the matches were over, as many as 500 people dashed to the 'dressing room' in a frantic scramble for their clothes. It was absolute mayhem. Everyone was feeling in the dark through a huge pile of clothes searching for his own. There was mud everywhere and the place smelt of a mixture of beer and perspiration. Somehow, though, everybody seemed to end up wearing the same garments as they took off.

This method of changing for football matches seems peculiar to the north of England. Grounds in the south usually have reasonable dressing room accommodation and certainly the pitches are flatter. No matter how frugal the changing conditions were or how uneven the pitch was, nobody lost his enthusiasm for the game.

Sometimes, though, players became a little over-enthusiastic. They took it as seriously, and played as keenly, as professionals in the FA Cup Final. As a referee, it was important to appreciate that. If any official was seen to be attempting to underplay or devalue a game, he would find little sympathy with the players, but occasionally they got carried away. Player problems are the single most frequent difficulty referees encounter at any level of football, and it was not unknown for players to remain angry long after the final whistle.

In one match I sent off a player – aged about eighteen or nineteen – and a few days later I was walking with my girlfriend and we decided to buy some fish and chips. We entered the shop in Sheffield Lane Top, close to where she lived, and were confronted by the same player. Only this time he had a few of his mates with him and they wanted to sort me out around the back of the shop. Not surprisingly, I declined their invitation, suggesting the match was over and the sending off should be forgotten. Fortunately, I emerged unscathed – perhaps the presence of my girlfriend saved me.

On another occasion I was refereeing the semi-final of the Sheffield Regional Sunday League between Ball Inn and Burncross 67 on the public works department's ground at Whirlow. Ball Inn won a fast, exciting match 2-1. The players were leaving the field at the end of the game when suddenly the Ball Inn goalkeeper and a spectator, who was supporting Burncross 67, started fighting with each other. The 'keeper picked up the branch of a tree and began swinging it furiously around his head and at the spectator.

A few players and I managed to separate the combatants and led the goalkeeper back to his dressing room. I obtained his name and sent a comprehensive report of the incident to the Sheffield and Hallamshire

County FA. I attended the hearing – the referee was never told the outcome and any punishment given – and some weeks later was surprised to discover that Burncross 67, the team that had lost the semi-final, were in the final of the competition. It transpired that the goalkeeper I had reported was, in fact, an ineligible player and Ball Inn had been disqualified for fielding him.

I thought I had enough problems when I refereed a match involving Sheffield Deaf. Obviously, they could not hear the whistle. So I carried a flag, blowing and waving simultaneously for the benefit of both teams when I wished to stop play. That was merely the beginning of an eventful afternoon.

The match went smoothly in the eyes of everybody apart from the Deaf team's opponents' centre-half. He committed a few fouls and generally made a nuisance of himself and I took his name. While I was shaking a few hands at the end of the game, the same player walked up to a lady with a pram standing on the touchline. They began shouting at each other in a fierce argument. Then the big centre-half struck the lady with sufficient force to knock her to the ground. We moved in and parted the couple and I was later amazed to hear that they were husband and wife. He received a fine and suspension on the evidence of my report.

A local referee called Brian Noonan was renowned for being fastidious about the condition of any pitch on which he handled a match. It was almost like an obsession. He wanted every pitch to look like Wembley. At least you knew that if you handled a game on a ground where Noonan had been the previous week, the pitch markings would be perfect. I was in charge of a game at Wadsley Church the week after Noonan had officiated there. Nevertheless, due to appalling weather, the pitch was almost unplayable. I would never have started a Football League match on it, but, with both teams willing, decided to give it a go.

We changed in a steel Nissen hut, which had no light, so we started as early as possible to enable us to see in the dressing room at the end of the match. It was another ground with a huge slope and, at half-time, the score was 5-3. Although the conditions were rapidly deteriorating, I decided to continue because the players were keen to finish. It was absolutely freezing. I was nearly suffering from frostbite and could not feel my numbed hands. Suddenly, for no apparent reason, one of the players started lashing out at everybody. Fists and feet were flying. He was eventually restrained and, in my report to the county FA, I said that he had a mental problem and had been affected by the intense cold, which was his team-mates' theory. I was attempting to defend him, to present a logical explanation for his behaviour. But a fortnight later, after I had refereed an inter-departmental match, I was confronted by this player and his father. They were most distraught that I had, they believed, questioned his sanity. Occasionally, trying to help players backfires.

Handling people on a football pitch has many similarities to handling people in work. It is all about man-management and it is no coincidence that many Football League referees are also successful businessmen. That might be the secret of dealing with the players during the match, but travelling to the ground can be a hazardous occupation in itself.

I used to referee matches on Christmas morning. Not having a car and relying on the vagaries of public transport during the festive season, I usually had to get up before eight o'clock to arrive in good time for an eleven o'clock kick-off.

A regular Yuletide appointment involved a complex journey from Grimethorpe, where I lived at the time, to Norton Woodseat's ground, incorporating two bus journeys and a long walk. This particular Noel morning was cold and ice had formed along the road. I was standing at the front of the bus, ready to get off, when suddenly, and for no apparent reason, the car in front of the bus pulled up sharply. The bus, skidding on the ice, careered into a bus shelter, totally demolishing it and damaging the front of the bus. I escaped unscathed, but shaken. Undeterred, I caught the next bus and went on to referee the match.

Once the referee has arrived in one piece at the ground, problems with players and changing facilites are not the only sources of difficulty. A proud groundsman and a broken crossbar provided the backdrop to two further memorable incidents in the early part of my career.

Jack was the groundsman at the Stocksbridge Works ground. He prepared a superb surface – lush green grass and neatly marked lines – and he was understandably proud of his pitch. Jack's pet hate was goalkeepers who, either before or during the match, rammed their boot into the ground around the goal area, usually either as marking for positioning purposes or to tee the ball up for a goal kick. He would enter the dressing room before each match and say, 'Hey ref, don't forget to warn the goalkeepers that they aren't allowed to mark the pitch.'

I managed to avoid arousing Jack's wrath by having a quiet word with the goalkeepers before the game. Once, though, on the Saturday after I had handled a match at Stocksbridge in the Yorkshire League, a 'keeper did it and Jack was so incensed that he ran onto the pitch and hit him. I

knew one or two goalkeepers who made marks on purpose, just to get Jack going.

I was handling an end-of-season match in the Sheffield and District Sunday League Premier Division. It was a top-of-the-table game, and whichever team won would be League champions. The score was 0-0 when a player shot at goal and the goalkeeper, leaping in an attempt to palm the ball over the top, succeeded merely in pushing the crossbar upwards and lifting it off its pegs. The ball struck the moving woodwork and bounced back towards the penalty spot, where the same advancing forward took a second shot. With three defenders on the line, there was total confusion as the bar landed on top of them.

My first reaction was to award a goal, because the ball had settled in what remained of the net. Fortunately, there were a couple of other referees, including Jim McMullen, an established local official, standing by the touchline. They quickly ran over shouting, 'No goal!' I decided to re-start the match with a drop ball. Afterwards, a succession of visitors came into my dressing room either congratulating or castigating me on my decision. But the laws state that the ball must pass between the posts and *under* the crossbar.

Another incident – involving an extraordinary coincidence – occurred one cold Sunday morning at Dronfield. A player jumped indiscriminately

with both feet at an opponent in possession with the clear intention of injuring him. However, with a twist of extreme justice, the result was that the player who had committed the offence was left writhing in agony on the ground clutching a broken ankle. The bone was visibly at an obtuse angle. I felt reasonably capable of dealing with the situation because I had undergone a six-week course in first-aid at night school. I believed this was necessary because medical help is rarely on hand at junior games. The referee should know how to deal with minor problems such as concussion and fractures and here was my first opportunity to put my knowledge into practice.

We secured the player's feet together, using his other leg as a splint, and kept him warm with hot water bottles and blankets, obtained from a nearby house, until the ambulance arrived. Nevertheless, the fact remained that this player was guilty of violent conduct. While he lay on the pitch, he admitted that he had been a 'bloody fool' and, indeed, had intended to inflict similar damage on his opponent.

I asked the player his name and address to pass on to the ambulancemen, and informed him that I would be reporting him to the county FA for violent conduct. One or two of the players thought I was being a little heartless and, perhaps, on reflection, I was. But the law states that violent conduct is a serious offence and I was following it to the letter.

After a delay of twenty minutes, I re-started the match. Almost unbelievably within five minutes, another player sustained a broken ankle. We went through exactly the same procedure – tying feet together and more hot water bottles and blankets. This time, however, the ambulance had still not arrived on the ground an hour after the second incident. When re-dialling 999, we discovered that the ambulance station thought that the second call was a duplication of the first. I abandoned the match and allowed everybody to change before there was further mishap.

4

Offside

Few subjects arouse greater debate among players, managers and spectators than offside. Was a player in an offside position when a goal was scored? Or, conversely, did the referee make the correct decision when he disallowed a goal for offside? It is not just a case of whether a player had two or more opponents between him and the goal line when the ball was released. There is the question of interfering with play and seeking to gain advantage.

A referee should learn the written word of the offside law and, with experience, he will develop the ability to judge interference and seeking to gain advantage.

A principal danger is that the referee and his linesmen will stop the game too frequently for offside. A player should not necessarily be penalised for offside just because he has fewer than two defenders or one defender and the goalkeeper between him and the goal line. A good official will not blow his whistle when there is clearly no question of interference or advantage being sought. He must study the position of the offside player when the ball was last played and decide.

There are a number of situations in which a player can never be given offside. A goal kick, for instance. If the ball is positioned on the ground within the goal area and the goalkeeper or another player kicks it cleanly into play and it reaches a colleague who does not have two or more opponents between him and the goal line, he is not offside. The laws state clearly that a player cannot be offside from a goal kick. However, and this is where the confusion comes in, if the goalkeeper punts a clearance from his hands and the ball travels directly to the same player in the same position, then he *is* offside. A goalkeeper kicking from his hand is, in effect, a normal outfield player.

A player cannot be offside from a throw-in, either. But again confusion can arise. If for example, a player takes a long throw-in and the ball is headed on by a colleague at the near post for another team-mate to head in at the far post in an offside position, the goal will be disallowed for offside. The scorer might claim that he can't be offside from a throw-in, but the ball did not go *directly* to the player in the offside position and the law which states that a player cannot be offside from a throw-in is negated as soon as another player touches the ball.

Often people ask me whether a player can be offside from a corner kick. The answer is no. If, after the kick has been taken, the ball goes directly to the centre-forward, who pops it into the net, that is fine and a goal is awarded. But if the centre-forward heads or shoots towards goal and one or more of his team-mates are on the goal line in an offside position, and clearly interfering with play, then a goal should *not* be awarded. The corner kick, as with a goal kick or throw-in is cancelled immediately another player touches the ball.

The question of interference frequently needs judging when players shoot at goal from long range. Remember in the 1981 League Cup Final at Wembley, when referee Clive Thomas allowed Alan Kennedy's goal for Liverpool against West Ham when the ball passed directly over the prostrate body of Sammy Lee? West Ham claimed Lee, in an offside position, was interfering with play. I think the defending team have a valid point if the offside player is directly in line with the shooter. If, however, a player is offside, but well out of the way of the shot, maybe near the edge of the penalty area, when a team-mate hammers the ball home from thirty yards, he cannot possibly be interfering. The goal should be awarded.

The same applies if the ball is kicked towards the right-winger, who is onside. But the left-winger or inside left might be offside. A judgement has to be made. Should a free kick be awarded for offside? The answer, in my opinion, is no. Those players on the opposite side of the pitch from the player with the ball are not intefering, and to halt the game causes an unnecessary interruption.,

Therefore, the linesman must learn to delay his flag-waving slightly. The left-winger might be offside when the ball is kicked, but it could go to the right wing. If he flags for offside, he has made an error of judgement. Linesmen should almost say to themselves, 'That's offside. One . . . two . . . three. He's interfering with play and now I'm going to flag.'

It is important that the linesman remains in line with the second rear-most defender. He can then judge whether players are offside or not

Diagram 1 *Offside* The Linesman (L) should remain in line with the second rear-most defender, ensuring that he maintains a clear 90° angle of vision

and also whether they are interfering *(See Diagram 1)*. The referee will rely on his linesmen quite considerably for those judgements. In the end, though, it is the man in the middle's job to decide whether a player is interfering and he should always be striving to keep the game flowing. Quite often during a match, a linesman will flag – he is indicating that a player is in an offside position – but the ball rolls safely to the goalkeeper or a defender. In this instance, I will see the opportunity for retaining the game's continuity and will not blow for offside. It is important that I acknowledge the linesman's signal, though, and show him that I am attempting to keep the game flowing.

One of the most difficult offside decisions to make is when a defending team use an offside trap that involves something akin to a cavalry charge up the field. Queens Park Rangers, on their fast-running plastic pitch, have often employed this method to catch the opposition offside and Wolves are among those teams who have practised the tactic in the past. It often looks as though a striker is a long way offside because, by the time the ball has reached him, he is maybe ten yards clear of the line of defenders. In fact, he might easily have been onside when his team-mate released the pass.

A piece of advice I would give to referees handling matches where there are no linesmen is: always blow for offside and ignore the question of interference. I remember having to sprint like mad when handling parks matches in an effort to get in line with the second rear-most defender so that an accurate decision could be made. I tended to blow for offside regardless of the position of the player. This, I discovered, caused fewer problems. Most players accepted that somebody was offside, but would start disagreeing if some were judged offside and others were not because 'he was or was not interfering with play.' A number of players did not understand the interpretation of nuances of the law regarding interfering with play, but they grasp the basic principle of a player being in an offside position.

Once a referee progresses to more major competitions, he will have linesmen. It is crucial then that he keeps them in view. He must patrol the pitch in such a way as to have wide vision of his linesmen, so that when the flag is raised it is seen almost instantly by the referee. He must attempt not to miss a linesman's raised flag. If he does not notice the flag and a goal results, then there is bound to be a problem. The referee will have to consult his linesman, who must always keep his flag aloft when a goal is scored, even if the referee has initially not noticed his signal for offside. If the resultant decision is the disallowing of the goal, players will be screaming that the decision was late. I will always ask my linesmen, both at half-time and at the end of a match, whether I missed any flags for offside.

When signalling offside, the linesman should first wave his flag vigorously and then, once the referee has blown, point it towards the pitch in a way that indicates the area in which the offside player was situated. The flag should be at an angle of about eighty degrees if the offside is on the far side of the field. If the player in the offside position is in the centre of the field, the flag should be held horizontal and, for an offside near the linesman, the flag is pointed towards the ground. These are rare occasions when the linesman should signal with his flag at anything other than forty-five degrees.

The referee should blow his whistle and make all his offside decisions in a positive and confident manner. Linesmen can help themselves and referees by getting into good habits. Quite apart from arriving at the ground early and listening to what the referee has to say, a linesman will improve his effectiveness when judging offside or other decisions and waving his flag by practising his signals. The best way to do this is to stand in front of a mirror with a flag, ideally in full kit, and change hands and put your arm at forty-five degrees and at other angles. You will then be able to appreciate exactly how good – or bad – your signals are in the eyes of the referee. If the arm is elevated too much, the flag will tend to hang down the shaft of the flag, lessening the area of material visible. The consequence will be that the referee will sometimes struggle to spot the flag. Do not be self-conscious – the more you practise, the better you will become.

Correct decision-making and signalling for offside by linesmen is not always a guarantee that things will run smoothly. Just occasionally, the unforeseen difficulty can be encountered. I was refereeing a match between Birmingham and Tottenham at St Andrew's a few years ago when, after just three or four minutes, the linesman quite rightly raised his flag for offside. Even though I blew the whistle, the player in possession, as they often do in this situation, ran through and kicked the ball into the back of the net.

When I looked at my linesman again to check the position of the free kick, he was still standing in the same place, but appeared in some difficulty. The Birmingham player, who had gone on and scored, was unhappy with the decision. Perhaps I had disallowed a perfectly legitimate goal, he hinted. I ran over to the linesman to discover what the problem was.

'The flag's come off the end of the stick,' he said.

I suggested that he should remain calm and obtain another flag – which he did and, in fact, he stayed admirably composed and put in a faultless performance for the rest of the match. I went back to the middle of the pitch and the players wanted to know the decision.

'Offside – no goal,' was my reply.

'Why didn't the linesman raise his flag?'

'He did, but the flag came off the end of his stick,' I said, attempting to pacify the situation.

'You know what he can do with the flag,' echoed the response. In fact, we all had a good laugh and the Birmingham players accepted the decision in the right spirit and without complaint.

One of the most contentious offside decisions I have given was in the first match I had been involved in that was covered by television, in my very early days as a linesman on the Football League list. Nottingham Forest were playing West Bromwich Albion, at a time when both clubs were in the Second Division. Roy Capey, a fit and respected Football

League official, was the referee and, as we walked out towards the centre circle at the start of the match, Roy joked, 'With the amount of hair-combing you've been doing in the dressing room, Keith, I suppose you want to run the line facing the cameras.'

'Of course,' I nodded, 'you're absolutely right!'

West Brom, playing some overwhelming football, went three goals ahead – thanks to a hat-trick by Ally Brown – and, with the game apparently sewn up, my mind started to wander. I started taking a few glances up towards the television cameras – how inexperienced I was in those days! I had already decided that I would be watching the game on television that evening, instead of going out for a meal or a drink, even though I was slightly disappointed that the cameras were not being pointed in my direction very often – all the play was in the other half.

Suddenly, though, I was confronted with a major decision. The ball had been switched to the Forest left-winger John Robertson, who was standing a yard inside the Albion half and in an offside position, and I raised my flag. But Roy Capey ran straight past, totally ignoring me. As the Forest players converged on the Albion goal, I was saying to myself, 'Please don't score, don't score.' For some reason, I glanced momentarily up at the cameras, half dropped my flag, and then put it up again. I remember thinking that I would not be watching *Match of the Day* that evening because I was likely to be 'crucified' by Jimmy Hill.

My worst fears were realised when Forest scored and the players began embracing in celebration. Roy awarded the goal but, as he was coming back to the centre of the pitch, he noticed that I was still standing there with my flag raised. I just wanted the ground to open and swallow me up, but there was no going back now. After consultation, Roy reversed his decision and the goal was disallowed. The crowd booed like mad and were very angry indeed.

Immediately after the re-start, I received a torrent of abuse and the crowd were generally questioning my parentage. I could handle the verbal insults – I had heard them all before – but when a beer can was hurled towards me, followed by a bottle, I became concerned. I did not want to be hit by a projectile, so I inched slowly down the line towards a policeman, who was sitting by the side of the pitch on a stool. I told him what was happening and that I needed protection.

He looked towards me, smiled slightly and then said somewhat agitatedly, 'There's no way I'm going to protect you. You've just dropped the biggest clanger of all time. That wasn't offside in a million years. You deserve all the insults you get.'

That evening, I took a deep breath and decided to watch the game on television. My decision to award offside was proved to be totally correct and since that day the presence of television cameras at a match has never worried me. I go out to run the line or referee and give what I believe to be correct decisions – regardless of whether millions of people will be watching from their armchairs.

Indeed, I have particularly poignant memories of one televised match which helped erase some sadness. It was between Aston Villa and Birmingham in December 1980. My father had died just a few days before the game and I was tempted to turn down the appointment. The rest of my family persuaded me to go ahead – it was what my father would have wanted, they said – and I did. It was a superb game and I received some kind praise from Barry Davies for my handling of the game and it helped me, in some small way, to overcome the problems I was facing at the time. Dad would have been pleased about that.

Offside decisions given by linesmen are not always going to meet with approval from the crowd. As they are closer than the man in the middle to the spectators, linesmen tend to receive more comments – some jocular, some barbed – than referees. The fans certainly did not have much that was kind to say to me after that disallowed goal in the Forest v Albion match, and I recall a game involving Johnny Grinsall, a former Football League linesman. Johnny, a pit deputy at Lofthouse Colliery, was a massive man, whose heart matched his physique. He was liked, respected and honest. On this particular occasion, Johnny was one of my linesmen and I was aware that he was receiving quite a lot of 'stick' from the crowd. All of a sudden, a ripple of laughter emitted from the spectators close to where Johnny was and I could see him smiling, too. After the game, I said, 'Come on, John, what was going on over there?'

'Well, I was getting a lot of stick from the crowd,' said Grinsall, 'and when one guy gave me some abuse, I suggested to him that running the line was, perhaps, not my best hobby. I've got five kids at home.'

5

Is the Match on, Ref?

I arrived at Grimsby's Blundell Park ground at eight o'clock in the morning. The pitch was rock-hard, covered with snow and that afternoon's match against Brentford was in jeopardy. Frank Bridge, the groundsman, was working frantically in an effort to get the pitch fit.

After consultation with Frank, I was sitting in the club's office, still undecided whether I should postpone the game, when the telephone rang. Nobody else was present, so I answered it. The voice at the other end belonged to the station superintendent at St Pancras, who said, 'I've got a trainload of hooligans here wanting to know whether the game is on or off. I've got to know soon, otherwise the train is not going to run.'

'The referee is still inspecting the pitch,' I said, 'ring back in a few minutes.'

I simply could not make up my mind. The Brentford team had travelled on Friday and were staying in a local hotel and Frank thought there was a chance of the match going ahead. I really put the pressure on him, saying, 'Look, if I give the game the go-ahead, be it on your head if the pitch is not fit by three o'clock.' Frank did a superb job, working from the moment I arrived right up until kick-off time.

I recall George Kerr, the Grimsby manager, walking gingerly across the pitch and demanding, 'Well, ref, is the match on?' I told him it was, trying to sound as convincing as I could. The game was played in a tremendous spirit, none of the players even hinting that it should not have started. There was an occasional problem when the snow cleared in patches and exposed the frost. I understand the Brentford fans travelled from St Pancras and arrived at Blundell Park in time for the match.

Deciding whether a game can go ahead in inclement weather is one of the most difficult decisions a referee has to make. If, for a Saturday game, there is any doubt, the referee will be on the telephone to the secretary of the home club as early as the Thursday. If no firm decision can be made then, the pair will speak again, often more than once, on the Friday. As referees often have long journeys to make for their Saturday appointments, a local official might be brought in to examine the pitch. By Friday evening, though, the match referee and club secretary will have decided whether the referee should travel, stay overnight at a local hotel and go to the ground first thing on the Saturday morning. An early decision – that is by Friday afternoon – will save on travelling expenses for the away club, if they have a long way to travel and an overnight stay, and spectators.

The two principal considerations when inspecting a ground are the safety of the players and the safety of the spectators. A game cannot go ahead if a pitch in perfect condition is surrounded by ice-covered terraces. When arriving at the ground, a discussion with the club secretary and the groundsman and a telephone call to the local meteorological office is followed by the actual inspection of pitch and ground.

The four most common weather conditions that cause the postponement of football matches are frost, snow, rain and fog. Frost is the most frequently disruptive and probably the easiest decision of the four for a referee to make. A frosty pitch that has not been rolled immediately after the previous game is almost certainly going to be unplayable. If the pitch is frosted and rutted, and there is little evidence that a thaw is imminent, then I will call off the match.

However, even the problems presented by frost can sometimes be overcome by improvisation. I was due to handle the Watford versus Nottingham Forest League Cup semi-final, second leg in 1979. There had been frost and freezing temperatures for the past few days and the prospects looked bleak. But both Watford and Forest had cluttered fixture lists and were anxious to play the match if at all possible, so Watford purchased bundles and bundles of straw and, with the aid of club officials, supporters and even players, were able to cover the Vicarage Road pitch to a depth of eighteen inches. The straw prevented the frost penetrating through to the grass and the game was played.

Occasionally, and especially in minor soccer, the referee can assist in making sure the match goes ahead. I remember one cold and frosty morning travelling to referee a match involving Black Bull Taverners at their Whitley Lane ground. At the time, I did not have a car, so for this Sunday morning fixture that was due to kick-off at eleven o'clock, I had to leave home at 8.30. The changing facilities comprised an old railway carriage, with the referee tucked away in one corner. I had caught a bus and managed to arrive at the ground at about ten minutes to ten. The pitch was frostbound, but I thought the game could go ahead if some of the bumps – particularly in the middle of the pitch and near each goalmouth – could be removed. I looked around and saw a large roller that was used in the summer for cricket. Rather than stand around getting extremely cold, I used the slope to help me roll the pitch in an effort to get the bumps down. The following week, in the *Sheffield Star*, there was a report saying that, not only had I refereed the match, but I was also principally responsible for it being played in the first place!

Pitches waterlogged by heavy rainfall can often be rendered playable by a conscientious groundsman. A playing surface almost completely under water at nine o'clock in the morning might be acceptable six hours later. Spiking is the most effective means of expediting drainage and it is amazing how quickly some pitches absorb water. It helps, of course, if the pitch was not already muddy, cut up or wet before the downpour.

I cannot remember more torrential rainfall than that which caused me to suspend the North American Soccer League match between New York Cosmos and San Jose Earthquakes on the Astroturf at New York's Giants' Stadium in 1982. The cloudburst was so severe that, within twenty minutes, an inch and a half of water covered the pitch. I brought the players off – much to the disgust of the spectators, who appeared to be enjoying the farce – and yet, almost as soon as the rain ceased, the pitch was clear of water. In England, it is highly unlikely that a referee would ever take the players off for rain and then recommence the game, but the Astroturf surface concealed a complicated drainage system. It does show how quickly surface water can disperse, but of course if it is raining, more rain is forecast and the pitch is already waterlogged, then the situation must be monitored with particular concern.

The depth of snow lying on a pitch often determines whether a game should proceed. One criterion here is that, if a ball is rolled across the pitch and gathers snow, in effect becoming a giant snowball, the match must be postponed.

Clubs sometimes advise me that they intend enlisting local supporters to help clear the pitch of snow. This, though, takes a long time and is not usually something that can be done in a matter of three or four hours. It can also be counter-productive. A pitch cleared of snow on a Friday is exposed to the elements and may become frosted overnight. Snow often acts as a 'blanket' over the pitch. Remember, a pitch with a layer of snow is often playable, while a frosted one is almost always unplayable.

I called off an FA Cup tie between Southend and Liverpool one Saturday a few years ago. Around eight or nine inches of snow covered the Roots Hall pitch. I arrived the following Wednesday evening for the re-scheduled match and discovered the pitch in perfect condition. The groundsman had done a magnificent job. The crowd flooded into the ground and there must have been more than 30,000 spectators present when Mike Dimblebee, one of the linesmen, entered our dressing room. He was covered with snow. I simply could not believe it and, when I donned my coat and went out to the middle to investigate, I discovered the pitch, too, was under a layer of snow.

I immediately asked the groundsman to start brushing the snow off the white pitch markings. But he was fighting a losing battle – the snow was coming down faster than he could clear it. I then decided we should allow the snow to lie on the field and asked the groundsman to mix a red dye with which he could re-mark the lines. The red of the dye combined with the white of the snow to produce a fetching pink colour. Patches of grass began to appear. Pink on green is not readily noticeable. Each of our best-intended procedures was being overtaken by the weather and it happened again when the snow once more began falling heavily.

Now the dilemma was: should the match go ahead? The pitch itself was touch-and-go, but there were other considerations. For instance, how

...IT'S NOT A SNOWMAN...IT'S THE REF INSPECTING THE PITCH!

much of a hazard would be presented by 30,000 disappointed people, who had all paid to travel to and get into the ground, leaving at once? Could the police usher them safely to their transport? The Liverpool team, and their supporters, had travelled down for the match – another postponement would incur further costs. Southend would have to pay turnstile operators, programme sellers, stewards, catering companies and the like – even if the game was now postponed. And, as a final consideration, the match was being televised by the BBC. You can see why clubs and referees like to decide whether a game should go ahead well in advance.

The managers, Dave Smith of Southend and Liverpool's Bob Paisley, kept in close touch and, when I decided to give it a try, I received their full support. The snow was so thick that, when I tossed with the captains for choice of ends or kick-off, the coin sank in the snow. I shouted 'heads' – not knowing whether it was heads or tails. The players from both teams adopted a very positive approach and the game was completed successfully.

On another occasion I received strong criticism in the local newspapers from Hartlepool chairman Vince Barker after I postponed a match they were due to play against Rochdale. I had passed the Victoria Ground fit at nine o'clock on the morning of the match and the Rochdale team began their journey across the Pennines. There was further snowfall in the early afternoon and this time, after a second inspection, I deemed the pitch unfit. The Rochdale team, whose coach became stuck on the motorway, arrived at the ground only to discover the match was now postponed.

Mr Barker, whose principal worry was that Hartlepool had developed a backlog of fixtures, admitted, 'I appreciate the problems with ice and I wouldn't advocate playing on a dangerous surface, but I think referees are being a little namby-pamby.' Mr Barker, in fact, struck the nail on the head. No referee likes changing his decision. After my morning inspection, I considered the pitch playable, but the subsequent snowfall rendered it dangerous. I am sure Mr Barker would not have been too impressed if one of his team's players had suffered injury because of the treacherous state of the ground.

The problem with fog is that it can come and go so quickly. In professional matches, the test I use is to ask one of my linesmen or a club official to stand between the posts of one goal. I then walk the full length of the pitch and go to the back of the stand at the opposite end of the ground. If I can still see the linesman, I am happy for the game to go ahead. In junior football, I will permit the match to proceed if, when standing on the halfway line, I can see both goals.

The speed with which fog can appear and then disappear was shown when I was refereeing an evening match in the Northern Premier League between Mossley and South Shields (now Gateshead). With twenty-five minutes remaining, a thick fog descended on the ground. I could not even see my linesmen and, after attempting to continue in these conditions for ten minutes, decided to halt the match. My intention, really, was to call it off. As I was leaving the field, a spectator came up to me and said, 'Hey, ref, can I give you a bit of advice? This could well be a hill mist and not necessarily fog. It could be nothing more than a cloud coming over the hills and temporarily affecting visibility. Why don't you give it a few minutes?'

I decided to bow to the man's superior local knowledge, but when I entered both dressing rooms, I was greeted with looks of amazement as I said to the players, 'Look, fellas, let's give it ten minutes. We may be able to re-start.'

'You must be joking,' came the stunned replies. 'The ref's gone mad.'

Sure enough, after about seven or eight minutes, the hill mist cleared and perfect visibility was restored. I received a lot of pats on the back after the game, when really all the praise should have gone to the spectator.

Just occasionally, wind can force soccer matches to be postponed. The main problem is that the force of a wind fluctuates. In the case of snow, frost and rain, the poor conditions are virtually constant. It is normally possible to predict some time before the scheduled kick-off that the pitch will be unfit. A wind can come and go within minutes. I have never had to postpone a Football League match due to gales and it would take a brave man to do so. I would certainly never call off a game in the morning and, in fact, the reason for postponing a match in such circumstances would probably be that the wind was causing another problem – blowing the roof off the stand, for example.

I did abandon a match once, though, due to wind. I was handling a game at Concord Park, Sheffield, some years ago. The pitch was on the side of a hill and there was a hell of a gale blowing. I stopped one of my two watches whenever the ball went out of play and let the other one run. Forty minutes had elapsed since the kick-off and yet we had had just nine minutes actual playing time. The ball kept being blown to the bottom of the hill. It was a mockery and the players were becoming fed up chasing the ball down the slope. They kept looking at me and nobody disagreed when I said, 'That's it, fellas, we're going home.'

With experience, a referee learns what to look for and how best to assess the situation when deciding whether a game should be played. Do not rush into a decision, but be aware that one should always be made at the

earliest possible moment. Be positive. It is no good just holding a moist finger in the air to find out which way the wind is blowing. Look at the pitch, the stands, the entrances to the ground. Consult the club secretary, the groundsman and met office. Consider the position of the police and the likely costs incurred as a result of your decision. I am in constant contact with the Football League or Football Association, depending under whose auspices the game is being played, relaying my findings to them. In the end, though, it is my decision.

Nothing gives me greater disappointment than having to postpone a match. I might have travelled a long way to get to the ground and have been looking forward to the game all week. Players, too, hate not playing – they have been working all week to prepare for the match. For supporters, 'Saturday's game' is often the main topic of conversation. Postponed matches can be financial ruin for clubs. Everybody involved wants games to go ahead. So I always feel a great sense of responsibility when I am asked, 'Is the match on, ref?'

6
American Experience

Seattle Sounders were winning 2-0 towards the end of the first half and in complete control when the crowd suddenly began shouting, 'We want Fish! We want Fish!' The feeling in the chants was so intense that I thought, 'This guy Fish must be a hell of a player.' During the half-time interval, I glanced at my teamsheet and noticed no player called Fish. I panicked a little. If Fish is brought on as substitute, I thought, I will have problems afterwards with a team fielding an illegal player.

As the second half progressed, the chants continued with even greater fervour. 'We want Fish!' echoed from the crowd, 'We want Fish!' Gradually the crowd's mood changed from enthusiasm to agitation. Boos and a torrent of abuse greeted the final whistle, even though Seattle had won 2-0. My linesmen and I agreed in the dressing room that the manager might have been better served bringing on Fish to satisfy the crowd and standing the consequences.

About an hour after the conclusion of the match, I was chatting with my eldest son, Paul, who had been in the crowd.

'A shame the fans didn't get their fish,' he said.

'They seemed pretty angry he wasn't brought on,' was my reply.

'Brought on? What do you mean, dad?' Paul asked with incredulity.

'Wasn't Fish the name of their substitute?'

'No,' laughed Paul, 'the crowd was shouting "we want fish" because, if Seattle won by three clear goals, every fan would have been issued with a voucher entitling him or her to a free meal at a local fish restaurant.'

The game took place in Seattle Sounders' massive indoor stadium in America, the land of sporting razzmatazz, during my two-month visit to officiate in the North American Soccer League in the summer of 1982. Soccer in the States varies considerably from the game in Britain and the

51

hectic trip filled a gaping hole in my refereeing education. In just eight weeks in America I stopped a match because of paper aeroplanes thrown from the crowd, wrapped my feet in aluminium foil, saw fans offered the opportunity to win a million dollars, had people deliberately throwing bottles at me, saw barbecues in clubs' car parks, head-butted a chicken, showed a spectator the red card, refereed on plastic pitches and was introduced to the crowd. In the States, ball game is carnival time, and it applies as much to soccer as to baseball, American football and basketball.

I was invited to America by Keith Walker, a former FIFA referee and one-time secretary of Sheffield United, but now supremo of the NASL officials. P.C. Henderson Ltd, my employers in England, granted me an eight-week sabbatical and, following careful deliberation with my family, who joined me for the final fortnight, I decided to accept the invitation. I received 180 dollars per game when refereeing, ninety dollars when linesman, thirty dollars a day meal allowance, twenty-five dollars a week for laundry, plus all travelling expenses.

I flew out of Heathrow on 5 June 1982 and was met by Keith at JFK Airport in New York. I returned to England on July 31 after having officiated in eighteen matches (the last seventeen as referee) and with many unforgettable memories. George Courtney, that excellent referee from Spennymoor, had told me that his visit to America improved his refereeing, especially in the area of man-management. George was right.

I was booked in the Doral Inn Hotel in Lexington Avenue and, upon arriving in the 'Big Apple', I was stunned by the awesome Manhattan skyline and struck by the sheer intensity of the noise level. The day after arriving, I saw my first American soccer match at the Giants' Stadium, New Jersey, when New York Cosmos played Toronto Blizzard. The quality of play and refereeing of Ed Bellion, an English-born lecturer at Texas University, was high. On Monday, June 7, I visited the League headquarters in the Avenue of the Americas to confirm my itinerary and collect a thick book of airline tickets, and I obtained my social security number from the local office.

Jacksonville was my next stop, and on Tuesday, June 8, I officiated in my first game – as linesman to Gordon Arrowsmith, a Scot resident in Toronto – between Jacksonville Teamen and Portland Timbers. Although an evening kick-off, the heat was grilling and I was continually being handed drinks. I was worried about being able to cope with the heat when I refereed my first game the following day.

I was driven by police car from the Harbour Hotel in Tampa to the ground, through the gates and onto the pitch. I walked back to the dressing room, changed, filled in the necessary forms and then, twenty minutes before the start, referee number eight (every referee in America has a number for the season and that was mine) was introduced to the crowd. So were the linesmen and the teams. All to a continual accompaniment of music and dancing cheerleader girls. Just before kick-off, the crowd rose and sang God Bless America. Within a few minutes of the start, I was used to the running commentary being given over the public address system. Every time the opposition gained possession of the ball, there was silence, while a cacophony of sound and music greeted the home team's every touch. The *William Tell Overture*, being played by a man on the organ, was the most popular tune and increased in velocity and decibels as the home side neared goal. Once, when I blew for a free kick for offside, the organ player struck up a chorus of *Three Blind Mice*. The crowd loved it.

My schedule was very tight. Not only was I handling matches, often 'back to back' (their expression for on consecutive days), I also conducted lectures. I experienced extremes of temperatures. One game, between Vancouver Whitecaps and New York Cosmos, was played in cold weather and a deluge. My next appointment was in Tulsa, where the temperature was well in excess of 100 degrees. After examining the Astroturf pitch, I returned to the dressing room where, to my amazement, I saw the linesman, having put on his socks, wrapping his feet in aluminium cooking foil. He said the metal reflected the heat and helped keep his feet cool. I did the same and it appeared to work.

This match, my first in Tulsa, introduced me to another 'first'. The heat and humidity caused enormous perspiration and a danger of dehydration, so it was important to consume liquid to maintain the body's fluid level. But when I was struck by a flying bottle, I turned in anger towards the boy who threw it, thinking he disagreed with one of my decisions or was just a plain hooligan. Then one of the players told me the bottle was for me to drink from. It is common practice in American soccer for feeding bottles – similar to those used by cyclists – to be thrown on to the pitch for players and officials in extreme heat.

One of the principal differences between American soccer and the game in Britain is that most matches over there are played on Astroturf. It took me a couple of games to acclimatise fully to the synthetic surface, and even these plastic pitches vary considerably. The one at New York's Giants' Stadium is a flawless surface, superbly flat and true, but the pitch at the Olympic Stadium in Montreal is old and, as a result, has deteriorated. At certain points on the carpet, where there are joins, the edges have curled up and this presents a hazard to the players. Some of the teams – like Jacksonville and Tampa – still play on grass and I must admit I remain a traditionalist. Football is a game that should be played on grass.

Another facet unique to the American game is the 'time-out'. This occurs whenever a player is injured or a break occurs in the game and is almost exclusively for the benefit of television and radio, on which virtually all the matches are covered. The referee raises his hands above his head and crosses them to signal a 'time-out' – a minute-long break in the game during which the television companies and radio stations broadcast advertisements. After the mandatory minute, a circular movement of a raised finger and a blast on the whistle re-starts the game.

Then there is the dreaded 'shoot-out'. No game in America ends in a draw. If the scores are level, the 'shoot-out', in which players have five seconds to run with the ball from thirty-five yards, shoot and attempt to beat the opposing goalkeeper, decides the winner.

The plastic pitches, combined with the heat and humidity, make it easy to collect blisters. I always ensured my feet and shoes were well-greased to prevent chafing. Liquid intake is important and so, too, is diet. I remember being taken round the Yonkers (Italian quarter) area of New York City by Vincent D'Ablis, the Italian assessor for the game I had taken between Cosmos and Vancouver. Keith Walker warned me not to indulge in too much spaghetti.

We walked past a small baker's shop, where a man was making huge cakes, about four feet in diameter and eight feet high. Apparently he supplied many of the best hotels in North America with wedding, birthday and other cakes. Vincent and I went to a bar where we met a number of other Italians and spent an enjoyable evening talking football. It was during the World Cup finals in Spain and, at the time, Italy had played their three opening group matches, in which they scraped draws against Poland, Peru and the Cameroons. They were somewhat fortunate to progress to the next stage and even these normally ebullient Italians were pessimistic about their chances. But, of course, Paolo Rossi and company were to prove them gloriously wrong.

We talked about English, American and Italian football and they well remembered players such as Denis Law, John Charles and Jimmy Greaves going to Italy in an effort to extend their careers. At the end of the evening, they offered to run me back to my hotel and, as a matter of interest, we would go via the Bronx. Before setting off, we checked that all the car doors were locked and windows closed and resolved not to stop at traffic lights, even if they were red. Although it was almost two o'clock in the morning, there were people everywhere. It was similar to how parts of America are portrayed in those films and plays of the Deep South, with people sitting on the steps near the streets in the middle of a hot and sultry night. The contrasts in New York were amazing. There were abundant signs of wealth – expensive cars, big houses, tall buildings – and yet, just a few miles away, off Fifth Avenue, here were people attempting to scrape a living.

Another 'first' occurred during the 'fish' match at Seattle – a woman linesman. Betty Ellis, a married lady with, I understand, five children, operates regularly in the NASL. Her ability puts some of her male counterparts to shame, although the general standard of officialdom across America is high.

Quite apart from usually being televised, every match in the NASL is video-taped. The tapes are immediately put on an aeroplane to New York, enabling Keith Walker, and the rest of the League's management committee, to observe any incidents and take necessary action. As in England, each match is watched by an independent assessor, who sends a copy of his report to the referee.

During one summer, I was certainly involved in my fair share of incidents. While the eyes of the footballing world were focussed on the World Cup finals in Spain, the American season was in full swing, and that usually means plenty of action.

One of the features of the American game is the wide diversity of nationalities among the players. Included in these are a number of British players, whose football education was gained from playing in the Football League, and it was English players involved when the Canadian local 'derby' game between Portland Timbers and Edmonton Drillers exploded on July 14.

Ron Futcher, the former Chester, Luton and Manchester City striker, knocked out an opponent with a tremendous right-hand punch. I immediately showed him the red card to eject him (the American for send off) from the field. As Futcher was walking off, Peter Mellor, the old Burnley and Fulham goalkeeper who had been substituted earlier in the match, ran across and attempted to become involved with Futcher. I managed to jump between them and prevent blows being exchanged, but, while my back was turned, John Pratt, the ex-Spurs player and now the club's youth team coach, swung a punch at Mellor. After consultation with my linesman, Pratt, too, was ejected. At seven o'clock the following morning, I received a call from Keith Walker, who told me he had seen the tapes of the match and that my actions were correct.

Another flare-up occurred at the end of a game between Chicago Sting and New York Cosmos. The match had been hard-fought, though never vitriolic, but as the players were leaving the field, Cosmos' Caesar Romero fell to the ground clutching his face. As the Chicago players were walking off in a different part of the ground, it was clear Romero had been punched by one of his own team-mates, although I had no idea who the offending player was. When Romero came round, he jumped up and ran towards Giorgio Chinaglia, the New York number nine and their star player, shouting, 'I vill kill him! I vill kill him!' Myself and a number of Cosmos players got between Romero and Chinaglia to ensure no further blows were exchanged. Apparently, Chinaglia was annoyed because Romero had not passed the ball to him throughout the match.

As I followed the players into the tunnel, I could hear that the fighting had recommenced in the dressing room. My linesmen and I decided to enter the room. I insisted Romero came out and he eventually ended up in the officials' dressing room with myself, the two linesmen and the assessor. We shared the showers and the player was eventually escorted back to the Hyatt Hotel, in which the team was staying. I, too, was booked into the Hyatt in downtown Chicago. A couple of hours after the match, the linesmen and myself went for a beer. At the other end of the bar, there were Romero and Chinaglia, sharing a drink and a laugh. Their fight had been completely forgotten.

My confrontation with the San Diego Chicken is not the type of thing that happens every week on the pitches of the Football League. Toronto Blizzard were at home to Vancouver and, when I blew for a free kick

against Toronto, the crowd started to boo. Suddenly, this character, with scrawny legs about three inches in diameter and dressed as a chicken, ran onto the pitch and presented me with a scroll, which, when unrolled, proved to be an eye-test chart. Apparently, he was quite well-known in the area. Ray Hankin, the former Leeds striker, who was playing for Vancouver, advised me to keep out of the chicken's way and not to get involved.

This human poultry was running around the pitch, generally attempting to poke fun at the players and officials and receiving roars of laughter from the crowd. However, after almost two minutes delay, I was concerned that the match might never get re-started. Something had to be done, I thought. I moved towards the chicken and shouted loudly, 'Will you please leave the field.' But the chicken had a huge polystyrene head and clearly could not hear what I was saying. I had to get closer. But, as I moved nearer, my head collided with his beak and he went flying, finishing on his back with his legs in the air. The crowd went berserk because I had head-butted their favourite San Diego Chicken.

Another game, between Vancouver Whitecaps and New York Cosmos, was played in atrocious conditions. After half-time, I went out to be confronted by an over-exuberant fan jumping up and down and performing a series of callisthenics in the pouring rain. He simply would not budge. So I showed him the red card and he walked, head bowed in mock shame, from the pitch. It brought the house down.

I almost did not referee my last game in America. I was already pushed for time when I left my hotel and caught a taxi to the Giants' Stadium for

New York Cosmos' evening match against San Jose Earthquakes. Driving through the Lincoln Tunnel, we came to a total standstill. There had been an accident ahead of us and we were stuck, unable to move forward or turn round to go by an alternative route. I sat there, anxiously watching the minutes tick away. The taxi was delayed for more than an hour before the debris was cleared. I eventually arrived about forty-five minutes before kick-off, although I usually like to have at least two hours at the ground before a match. Fortunately, my senior linesman Ben Fusco, a Canadian FIFA official, had taken care of the referee's responsibilities relating to the team sheets. I received some stern glances from the San Jose coach, who was unhappy that I was handling the game in the first place. In fact, he was the only person who voiced his disapproval at my refereeing in America.

Carlos Alberto, who led the great Brazilian team to their World Cup triumph in 1970 and was captain of New York in this match, had also been stuck in the Lincoln Tunnel. Professor Mesai, the Cosmos coach, requested that I stall the kick-off to give Alberto time to appear. I rejected this proposal, stressing that NASL rules stated that the teamsheet had to be in by a specific time, fully aware, of course, that I had been late myself. I insisted Alberto missed the match and an alternative player was named.

During the course of the game, which was covered live on television, there was an almighty downpour and within minutes more than an inch of surface water covered the pitch. It was impossible to play the ball, so I suspended the match. The television company, who were continuing their broadcast, asked me to inspect the pitch for the benefit of the cameras, which I did and received another soaking. Within five minutes of the rain stopping, the pitch, which had remarkable drainage, was fit for play and we were able to re-start and complete the game.

In another game involving San Jose, at home to Jacksonville, one of my linesmen failed to appear, so I had to call upon Dr David L. McGowan, the executive director of the Adult Independence Development Centre in Campbell, California, to take the flag. David, an international ice hockey referee, had little experience officiating in soccer, yet his performance was superb. It does just illustrate that a referee from another sport, with a 'feel' for taking charge of professional sport, can, when given careful instructions, quickly pick up the rudiments.

The Americans are brilliant at selling the game. The English authorities who complain about and wonder at dwindling attendances should take a crash course from the Americans, the masters of hard-sell. The NASL fan watches in luxury compared to his English counterpart, who can get soaked and freezing on the terraces and struggle to get a cup of Bovril. The English rely on soccer, the ninety minutes of the game itself, to attract the crowd. To the Yanks, the match is merely the focal point of a cavalcade of stunts designed first to draw and then to entertain the spectators. And free fish, music, and pretty dancing girls are just the start.

They work hard at getting people, and particularly families, into the stadium. For instance, Chicago Sting persuaded various companies to sponsor five games they thought unlikely to attract high attendances. The first 10,000 people to turn up at the first match received a pair of soccer stockings in Chicago's colours at the expense of a drinks company, who, of course, in turn received maximum exposure. For the next game, another company sponsored pairs of shorts. Then shirts . . . hats . . . scarves. After five games, people could be completely kitted out in Chicago Sting regalia – but only if they had been to the ground.

Most clubs usually had bands playing and barbecued food available in the car park prior to the match. It was not uncommon for people to arrive three or four hours before the start. Tickets for the next home game were constantly being offered as prizes in lotteries, competitions, games and the like. At half-time, there is invariably some form of entertainment. I remember one game in Toronto, when the Blizzards were playing Vancouver Whitecaps, in which spectators were invited to fold paper aeroplanes and attempt to throw them into large bins on the pitch. Those who succeeded won prizes. But it was raining and, as we came out for the second half with half the pitch covered in paper planes, I had to delay the re-start. The players, who wore pimpled or even flat-soled shoes on the Astroturf, could hardly stand up.

In another competition, a car was placed on the halfway line and a piece of canvas with a hole not much bigger than a football attached to the goalposts. Spectators were invited to kick a ball over the car and bounce it through the hole. Not easy, perhaps, but the prize was not bad – a million dollars! Elsewhere, kids were invited to kick balls through a hole in a plastic sheet attached to the goalposts and win free doughnuts.

I accepted the offer to go to America for two principal reasons. The prospect of travelling round the country at somebody else's expense for two months, the last two weeks of which would be with my family, was very appealing. The other attraction was that I felt sure it would improve my refereeing. I received a warm welcome everywhere, being met at each destination by an NASL official and often staying with fellow referees. I spent two or three days at the home of Gordon Arrowsmith and his family in Toronto, Frank Jewel in Daytona, Peter Aradi in Tulsa and so on. I met my family in San Francisco on July 15 and then moved with them to Chicago, which, to my surprise, I liked very much and stayed with Ian Rutowski, an NASL linesman, and his wife, two Polish people who had settled in the States.

Constantly in the background, smoothing over any problems, were Keith and Brenda Walker. Keith's reputation was immense and many of the referees treated Brenda, who acted as Keith's secretary, like a second mother. She arranged my hectic itinerary and I developed a type of professionalism in flying, learning to arrive at the airport with the minimum amount of time to spare so I could go through the baggage procedures quickly and straight on to the aircraft.

Apart from the pleasures, I was convinced the trip to the States would improve my refereeing. So it proved, and no more, as George Courtney had predicted, than in the area of man-management. In America, a referee is handling international players from a variety of nationalities. Some understand what you are saying, others do not. Often, facial expressions or gestures with the hands are the only means of communication. But a referee *must* make himself understood. The sheer intensity of my schedule required me to be both physically and psychologically prepared.

There is no doubt in my mind that the 1982 North American Soccer League referee number eight returned home to England better at his job.

7

The Five Cs of Refereeing

A carpenter has chisels and a saw. A teacher has chalk and a blackboard. A doctor has a stethoscope and a thermometer. A referee has a whistle and a notebook. But it is no good having the tools of your trade if you do not know how to use them. A carpenter might require craft and precision, a teacher projection and patience, a doctor compassion and understanding. A referee needs the Five Cs to be good at his job. The Five Cs are control, communication, courage, consistency and commonsense. A man who can successfully encapsulate each of these five facets is an outstanding football referee. No official, when he walks out to handle a match, knows what problems he will encounter. Some will be familiar situations, others he will not have experienced previously. But correct application of the Five Cs will help ensure a smooth-running match.

It is important to recognise that football is about players – not managers, not chairmen and certainly not referees. At the highest levels, these men are paid huge sums to entertain an audience. Usually, that is all they want to do. But sometimes, players choose to pursue less acceptable objectives. Correct application of the Five Cs will help eradicate the likelihood of this happening. Occasionally, other problems nothing to do with players, such as crowd disturbances, will also require employment of the Five Cs.

Control A referee controlling twenty-two footballers is rather like an office manager controlling twenty-two clerks or typists. He must be seen to be fair, positive, diplomatic and to inspire confidence. It is all about man-management. It is important that the referee begins in the way he intends to continue. When the referee first stops the game, he is the focus of attention for the spectators, possibly the television viewers and, most of all, the players. They are waiting to see how he will react, how he will treat the situation. He must demonstrate immediately that he means to control the game effectively.

So, when the ball goes out of play for the first time or when the referee first awards a free kick, he must indicate clearly in which direction the throw-in or kick has been given. The palm of the signalling hand should be open-faced, giving good vision to the players. You might think it is a small point, but it is an important one. Players respond favourably to positive signals and decisions. The referee is trying to win their respect and he will be more successful if the players see that he is making his decisions in a positive manner, without prejudice, and is in harmony with his linesmen.

If a player attempts to gain ground at a throw-in or a free kick, three short blasts on the whistle or a word delivered by mouth can be used to make sure he takes it from the correct position. Failure to do so undermines a referee's control and the opposing players will either become irate or themselves attempt to take advantage of the ref's leniency.

A free kick from which there might be a shot at goal, usually just outside the penalty area and sometimes referred to as a 'ceremonial' free kick (not a term FIFA like referees to use) is a situation in which a referee needs to exercise tight control. Defenders are always attempting to encroach within the stipulated ten yards. If a referee allows encroachment, his problems will rapidly escalate. Some people might think that referees are being unduly pedantic by insisting that the 'wall' withdraws to the full ten yards. Why, they say, interrupt the flow of the game when eight yards will surely suffice? For a start, eight yards rather than ten, could mean the difference between missing the target with a shot and scoring a goal. Players nowadays are so expert at curling free kicks, that having the wall two yards nearer could prevent them finding the correct angle with their shot. The crowd might not think two yards makes much difference, but the players do. When it is the attacking team's turn to defend at a ceremonial free kick situation, they, too, will attempt to encroach. The problem will merely get worse unless the referee takes a firm line. Anyway, the laws of the game state ten yards.

The referee must quickly recognise whether the attacking team is going to take the kick quickly. If so, that is fine – as long as they realise that, if they take a quick kick and lose possession, that is bad luck. They are not going to have another chance. If it is a free kick close to goal and a defensive wall has been formed, then the referee must supervise players and do it positively *(See Diagram 2)*.

The first thing I do is take charge of the ball. It will be in my possession, allowing me to control the point from where I want the kick to be taken. If I

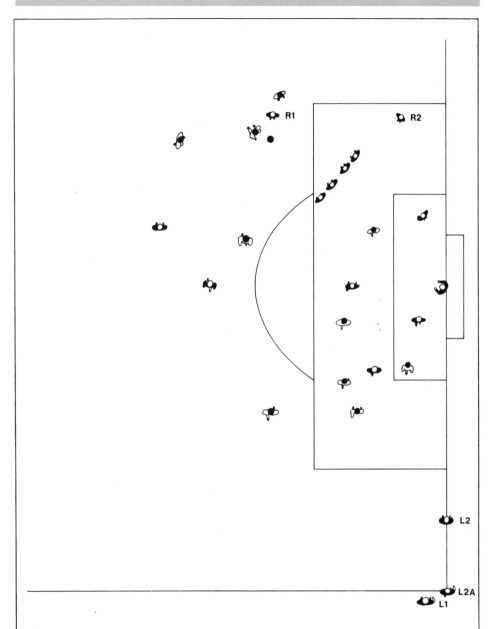

Diagram 2 *Free kicks close to the penalty area*   The referee supervises the position of ball and players (R1) before taking up position to observe potential problems with the defensive wall and to watch for offside (R2). The linesman checks initially for offside in case of a quick free kick (L1) and then, on a signal from the referee, moves to watch the goal line (L2 or, in European or FIFA games, L2A)

allow the attacking players to have the ball and I move away from the point of the free kick, they can move it three yards forward or three yards to one side to get a better angle for a shot at goal. I place the ball between my feet, literally standing over it. I do not recommend referees to put one foot on the ball – that leaves you off balance. So I stand over the ball, indicate that I want the defending players ten yards back in a complete circle and say to the attacking players, 'Don't kick this ball until I blow the whistle.' Once the wall is back ten yards, I take up the desired position for the kick to be taken. The referee should cover the offside and the linesman watch the goal line. An alternative used by some referees – including me at times – is to place the ball on the correct spot, tell the attackers not to kick or pick it up until the whistle is blown and then go to the side of the wall and work at getting the players to withdraw. A problem with this method is that there can be confrontations between opposing players on the far side of the wall, out of the referee's vision.

If players refuse to retreat ten yards, they must be cautioned to dissuade them from encroaching again at the next free kick. The referee must be aware of other practices – often encouraged by coaches – that give the attacking team an unfair advantage at free kicks. The kicker might start talking to one of his colleagues or the referee, asking him for ten yards, and, while the defenders' attraction is taken away from the ball, another player will run through and shoot for goal. The kicker could run up towards the ball, and when reaching it, stop and claim to the referee that the wall has encroached. While everybody is distracted, he chips at goal. Attacking players sometimes position themselves in the wall with the sole intention of creating a confrontation with their opponents. They will hold shirts or maybe tread on toes. Other attacking teams might say they are happy with the wall being seven yards away – allowing them extra space to play in behind it. A referee must understand that both attacking and defending teams are prepared to cheat to get the desired result, and he should always be consistent regarding the ten yards.

The whole question of ten yards is important in my opinion. I believe a referee's failure to insist on ten yards is representative of his lacking control. While I was in Mexico during the summer of 1983 for the World Youth Championships, a man who trains the Mexican Olympic athletes was appointed as the referees' trainer for the duration of the tournament. He took us above sea level to the forests. The altitude required referees to be physically fit to stand the pace and he devised various training routines that also necessitated mental alertness. In one, an area was created by driving broom handles into the ground. A number of referees were in this confined area, running and attempting to avoid bumping into one another. This improved manoeuvrability. We had to retain vision because different coloured cards, each with its own particular instruction, were shown. Red meant move to the left, yellow to the right and so on. We needed to keep one eye on these and the other on our colleagues – and looking at more than one thing simultaneously is a facility all referees need.

Another exercise was specially geared to improve our ability to achieve ten yards. We went out onto a pitch, where a ball was thrown. We took it in turns to act as referee in imaginary free kick situations. The other officials would form a wall, acting sensibly and retreating another yard or two when asked to do so. Initially, when measured with a tape, most of the referees had actually stationed the wall about seven yards from the ball when stating they would be satisfied with the distance in a match situation. Our judgement improved later. We were educated to use the pitch markings as a guide for ten yards. For example, the distance between the penalty mark and the arc is ten yards. So, when a free kick is awarded in that vicinity, a referee can use the markings to help him judge ten yards.

The World Youth Championships, incidentally, were won by Brazil, who beat Argentina in the final. I was the only English referee present, although Brian McGinley from Scotland also officiated. I refereed in two matches, Brazil v Russia in the early rounds, and the quarter-final between Argentina and Holland. The South Americans love their sport and the crowds at the matches were large and noisy.

If I give a free kick near the centre circle and a forward of the defending team runs up and stands close 'looking at' the ball, I am going to stress strongly to that player that I want him back ten yards. If players are allowed to encroach at a free kick in the middle of the pitch, you can rest assured they will attempt to when the kick is in the vital area around each penalty box.

Foul tackles require vigilant control. For example, if a forward with his back to the opponents' goal passes the ball to one of his team-mates, and, having released the ball, is brought down by a late foul tackle from behind by a defender, it is imperative that the referee takes action. The defender should be cautioned under the heading of ungentlemanly conduct. If the players feel that, having distributed the ball, they are not going to receive protection from the referee in these situations, they are likely to start protecting themselves – by reciprocal foul tackles or general retaliation. Do not allow an escalation of bad tackles. Advantage is all well and good to keep the game flowing, but it must not be allowed to put control at risk.

The 'over the top' tackle is an even more serious offence. In football terminology, this means that a player, instead of going for the ball, deliberately passes his foot above the ball and rams it into his opponent's shin. Some players attempt to use the ball as a 'decoy' in this type of offence. They brush the heel of their boot across the top of the ball – thus moving it – but still crash their boot into the leg of the opposing player. 'Over the top' tackles – whether or not the ball is used as a 'decoy' – should result in the offender being sent off.

There are potential flashpoints in the game that will result in a loss of control if the referee does not get hold of them. One of the most common flashpoints is the forward-goalkeeper confrontation. For example, a goalkeeper, having been fouled by a forward, might have retained possession of the ball in his hands. The referee signals 'play on' and, with the forward still harrassing him, the goalkeeper follows through with his leg – aiming for the forward – after punting his clearance. In this particular instance, it is often in the referee's interest to blow for the free kick and not to apply advantage. But if you have signalled 'play on' and the goalkeeper attempts to retaliate, make it known you are not going to stand for it. Move in and talk to both players. If a referee stands fifteen or twenty yards away, blows his whistle and then runs off, players will think they are not going to be protected by the official. Get in where the trouble is.

When defenders and forwards rise together to head the ball, watch carefully for offences. The defender might be 'climbing', placing an arm on the forward to prevent him from jumping, pushing in the back with the palm of the hand before the ball has arrived, sticking his knee into an opponent from behind, or holding his shirt. These all put the forward off balance and niggle him. The striker, on the other hand, realising he will not win the ball, could fall down pretending he has been fouled. Or he could back into or elbow a defender, or hold his shirt and spin off it. The forward might also stoop below the centre of gravity of the defender and back into him as if he was about to run off with the ball – attempting to con the referee into believing that the defender was 'climbing' and should award the forward a free kick. Escalation of these problems will cause a loss of control. Remember, do not fall into the trap of looking at the airborne ball – watch the players on the ground.

Another potential flashpoint occurs when a forward, with his team leading by one goal and just a few moments of the match remaining, runs towards the corner flag and stands over the ball in an attempt to waste valuable seconds, inviting defenders to have a go at him. It is vital for the referee to arrive on the scene quickly.

Dissent should not be permitted. People often tell me that they have seen a player escape without punishment for a dangerous tackle, yet receive a caution for nothing more serious than a comment to the referee. Surely, some officials have got their priorities wrong? My answer is that no official should take anything other than a dim view of foul play, but dissent and disparaging comments must also be eliminated. If a referee allows dissent, he is setting a dangerous trend and totally undermining his own authority and control.

There are two forms of dissent. One is the player who openly rejects a referee's decision. He does this by looking in an agitated manner at the referee, passing a comment, kicking the ball away or throwing it into the ground or, perhaps, ironically applauding a decision. The player is disputing the official's authority by actions or words and should be cautioned.

The other form of dissent comes from the player who is continually 'chipping away' at the referee. He is questioning every decision – not openly – but in a quiet, almost sly fashion. There is probably a reason for it – perhaps a penalty had been awarded against him or his team earlier in the game. He now wants to continue a dialogue, not necessarily with the referee, but maybe with his own team. Comments such as 'I think the ref is having a bad game today' or 'Don't take much notice of this referee because he's a bit behind the play and he's not really enjoying it' or 'He's a bit one-sided.' As much as anything, he is attempting to whittle away some of the referee's confidence and firm action must be taken. Tell the player that you are unhappy with his level of dissent and, if it continues, he will be cautioned.

Comments are not always directed at the referee. If the referee allows the banter between one player and another to develop to the point where it explodes, he has a problem. I attempt to step in with a quiet word before the flashpoint is reached. I might say, 'Look, fellas, I'm going to be the third man if you two don't behave' or 'Come on, pipe down and get on with the game. People have come to watch you play, not chat and have a go at one another.'

Referees can make errors when a player is injured. Firstly, it is important to ascertain whether the player is actually hurt. It is not unknown for players to feign injury, either to waste time or to get an opponent into trouble. If the trainer is summoned every time a player goes down, the match will lose all continuity. The trainer will be on and off the field like a yo-yo. So the referee has to take a fairly firm line with injuries. If the injured player is by the touchline, the treatment can often be administered off the field of play – especially if it is a leg injury – thus reducing the stoppage time.

It is in the area of head injuries where the referee has to exercise extreme caution. If I see a player sustain a head injury, I stop the match immediately. I remember that during the 1983 FA Cup semi-final between Manchester United and Arsenal, Kevin Moran, the United defender, suffered a serious-looking head wound. I was very close to Moran at the time and, indeed, caught him in my arms to prevent him falling to the ground as he collapsed. I blew the whistle immediately, even though one team was on the attack. Referees cannot afford to take risks in these situations. If I am going to err, I always err on the side of safety.

Once the trainer has come onto the pitch, the referee wants him off as quickly as possible. Quite often, referees – including myself a few years ago – meet the trainer as he comes onto the field and say, 'As quickly as possible, please' or 'Get the player off.' That is almost guaranteed to cause an argument, with the trainer concerned for the well-being of his player and angry that the referee is apparently more worried about re-starting the match. I now allow the trainer the time necessary to treat the player or remove him from the field. Most trainers, aware that a lengthy stoppage disrupts the flow of the match, take a sensible line.

How often have you seen a referee, when a player is down and the trainer has been summoned, leaning over and continuing to talk to the player until the trainer arrives? Obviously, the referee wants to know the extent of the injury, but he can leave it to the trainer to ask him, 'How are you?' or 'Where does it hurt?' We are expected to control twenty-two players and, therefore, I think it is important not to remain stooped over an injured player. It could be that he was hurt by a foul tackle and his colleagues are intent on seeking retribution. The referee should move about eight yards away from the injured player, allowing much better vision of the other twenty-one players. It is our job to control the majority, not to concentrate exclusively on an isolated, prostrate player.

Once the referee has blown for half-time or full-time, he should not relax his control. Indeed, when walking off, a referee and his two linesmen should be even more alert than usual. The officials must attempt to alleviate any possible frustrations and repercussions.

A referee in effect has to be a thermometer, measuring the temperature of each player. He must recognise a wise head, a player who has been in the game for a long time and is not quite as sharp as he once was. An experienced defender, for example, who has learned to be cunning over the years, might be up against a young winger, full of tricks and pace. The defender realises he will be in for a run-around unless he resorts to tactics such as holding the winger or issuing verbal threats. The danger here could be that the winger will suddenly crack and attempt retaliation. A quiet word with the older player, mentioning that you have seen his intentions, could be the answer. If the referee goes in 'full bore' with an aggressive attitude to sort out the problem, he often makes it worse.

Communication A referee has three means of communication – the whistle, his signals and his voice. We can develop skill in our use of the whistle. The less we blow it, the more effective it becomes when we actually need to use it to stop the game or attract attention. So I do not think there is any need to use the whistle when the ball goes out of play for a corner, goal kick or throw-in. The players know the ball is off the field and superfluous sounding of the whistle becomes irritating. A bad tackle requires a good, long blast so the players can detect the referee's annoyance merely from the way he blows his whistle. Short blasts can assist in control situations, such as supervising a free kick.

Difficulties – and often quite comical situations – can arise in junior football, when there might be a dozen or more pitches in the same field, often no more than a couple of yards apart. I have been handling a junior match when another referee, with a similar sounding whistle, blows loudly and brings four matches to a halt!

We must always be willing to communicate and sometimes a smile from the referee can take the heat out of a situation. We are communicating, of course, when we caution or send off a player, and I use the same procedure whether I am taking the name of the junior player in the park – in other words, a player whose name I do not know – or Bryan Robson. I make a note of the player's number as soon as possible as a definite means of identification and then say, 'I am cautioning you. What is your name?' I always use these words so as to be consistent. I write his name, his offence and the time in my notebook. Say, for example, F. Smith has been cautioned for a late foul tackle from behind after an hour, I would write: F. Smith, LFB, 60. DT means deliberate trip in my own form of soccer shorthand; DTFB is deliberate trip from behind and so on. There is no need to tell the player what he has been cautioned for. He usually knows his crime and the most frequent category is ungentlemanly conduct, which covers a variety of offences and means little to most players. All they know is that they have committed a foul.

In European matches, referees use red and yellow cards, on the back of which the offending player's number, name, offence and time is written.

They are something I am very much in favour of. The cards, which were used in the Football League for a few seasons, provide an excellent means of communication – not just to the player being punished, but also other players. They will think, 'Hey, this ref is not standing for any nonsense.' The cards also inform the spectators, Press, and everybody else that a player has been cautioned. As it stands in the Football League, with the current writing in the notebook method, it is not always apparent. I accept that waving coloured cards can make a spectacle out of an aspect of the game that should be underplayed as much as possible, but it depends on how the referee holds them aloft. Bad referees show the cards almost triumphantly or shove them under the noses of players as if they are enjoying cautioning or dismissing players.

Often a player who has committed a bad tackle will lie on the ground. He knows he is going to be cautioned and is just trying to stall for time. What the referee must not do is bend over him and declare, 'Right, I'm cautioning you.' If the trainer needs to come onto the pitch, wait for him to leave – remembering, of course, to stop the watch – allow the player to get up and then approach him. This way you can talk to him eye to eye.

I am a fairly big chap. If I go over and talk to a player, many of whom are six inches or more shorter than me, and stand over him, he will feel as if he is being overpowered. I want to talk to him without him having to look upwards. Having him staring at my chin does not lead itself to good man-management. So I will take a pace or two backwards, if necessary shouting louder, so that our conversation can be conducted eye to eye. I am attempting to use man-management to get a better response from players.

Sometimes the referee is as annoyed as the player when a caution takes place. It is crucial he does not show that annoyance. He must not enter a situation with a bombastic attitude. Cool and calculated, perhaps taking a little more time than necessary in order to give the player the chance to calm down. When I take a player's name, I make it quite clear that any repeat of the offence will mean his dismissal from the field, without sounding as though I am threatening the player.

Again, there is a standard procedure after a match in which a player or players have been cautioned or sent off. Forms are provided in which details of club, ground, date, player, and nature of offence are requested. These forms must be returned to the Football Association, County FA, FA of Wales or wherever appropriate as soon as possible. Linesmen need make a report only if asked to do so by a particular league, the FA or in the case of crowd misconduct. Reports of Football League matches are returned to the FA. The only items I must submit to the League are the two teamsheets.

I remember when black players first started appearing regularly in the Football League during the mid-seventies. They are commonplace now, of course, but some of them found it lonely and dispiriting on the pitch when receiving a lot of 'stick' from the crowd. I can remember giving them encouragement, not by telling them how good they were, but things such as, 'You are out on the field playing, and they're not. I'm quite sure they would rather be down here. Why don't you just show them what you can do with the ball.' This would be a private chat between the player and me, designed to relax him and avoid the consequences of his being frustrated.

The playing of advantage requires good communication, not just a clear shout of 'play on' and arm signals, but also because both the players involved must be spoken to. You do not have to march over to the man who has committed the offence there and then, but quietly inform him that you were unhappy with the action when the game next stops. At the same time, it is important for the referee to speak to the player offended against – he should be made aware that you saw the offence, but in this instance considered it more advantageous to his team to play on. Otherwise, a player on whom the foul count has been high, yet who is not being awarded many free-kicks because of the application of advantage, might suddenly protect himself by thumping an opponent. The referee could be to blame, because he has not told the player what he is trying to achieve.

Communication can also have its funny sides. I remember once approaching a player and looking and feeling quite annoyed because he was holding on to the ball, preventing an opponent from taking a throw-in. I ran up to him and suggested that he got rid of the ball, whereupon he threw it in my direction and said, 'Well, ref, you can have it, because we sure as hell don't know what to do with it!'

Courage A referee must have the courage of his convictions. If he sees what he thinks is a penalty, he should give it, no matter what the match or situation. Just ask Jack Taylor. He awarded two penalties in the first half of the 1974 World Cup Final between The Netherlands and West Germany. Do not let the crowd affect your judgement – have the courage and the confidence to do what you believe is correct. If a referee performs well, he can enhance a game. If he performs badly, he can ruin it – both for spectators and for players. Recognise that a game of football is in some respects like a game of chess – be patient, but when the moment to take action does arrive, have the self-belief to carry it out. Never, though, for the sake of it. Excessive use of the whistle and unwarranted verbal warnings are nauseating and, indeed, just as bad as being too lenient.

At the end of a match, when a manager wants to dispute one of the referee's decisions, the ability to walk straight ahead is not a lack of courage. Quite the opposite. A head-to-head confrontation at the conclusion of the game is inviting trouble. Allow the situation to cool with a comment such as, 'I'll see you later.' Players respect a referee who is confident in everything that he does. But never appear arrogant – footballers resent that.

Football League referees often required plenty of courage to enforce the new guidelines on the 'professional foul' during the 1982-83 season. Sending a player off, especially in front of a big partisan crowd, is never easy, but officials were instructed to dismiss offenders if a goalscoring opportunity was denied by a deliberate foul. The number of dismissals rose enormously. Whereas a sending-off was a disgrace, almost a scandal, in the immediate post-War years, we were now often getting ten or more in a week, but I believe the clampdown had the desired effect.

In the past, spectators were being deprived of what they had most come to see – shots at goal – because of the 'professional foul'. Since the clampdown, the number of goals has increased. The change in interpretation prompted a clean-up. I know some defenders complained that they were scared even to attempt a tackle for fear of being sent off, but the clampdown punished fouls, not clean tackles. The escalation in the number of sendings-off was not a good advertisement for the game, but it was acceptable when balanced against the increased attempts at goal. Anyway, players knew the consequences if they overstepped the mark. The hard-line interpretation of the laws has now been rescinded by the FA and FIFA, but we have not seen 'professional fouls' creeping back to the extent that they existed before, so I think it was a worthwhile exercise.

'Professional foul', incidentally, is not a term I like. It represents everything that is unprofessional about the game. 'Cynical' is a more appropriate word. We are attempting to get fairness in soccer. The physically stronger player should not always win the challenge. Skill should be the deciding factor.

Consistency Consistency is a vital attribute for a referee. Not just from match to match, but also throughout the ninety minutes. Managers and players complain often and loudly that there is inconsistency between different referees and by the same referee during a single match. All referees should indulge in self-analysis and consider whether they are being consistent in the accuracy of their decisions and actions.

Could any inconsistency, for example, be due to lack of fitness? All Football League referees undergo a physical examination at the start of each season but, as a referee tires towards the end of the match and consequently is farther from the play, so he suffers loss of consistency.

A decision given from ten yards away is more readily acceptable than one given from half a pitch-length away. A referee must work at positioning and fitness. It is important he is on the scene and appreciates the type of problems that might occur if he is not there. A fireman always gets as close as he can to put out the flames. He never releases the water from his hose from 100 yards away because, by the time it reaches the fire, it will be in small droplets. A referee, too, is less effective when a long way from the action.

Some people maintain that referees should 'hit them hard' in the first twenty minutes. Blow the whistle, stop the game, lecture players and take a couple of names so as to get a grip. Then, later in the same game, play the advantage freely. In my book, that is inconsistency. If a bad tackle results in a caution in the first minute, the same offence by another player in the last minute should also prompt a name being taken. If a player has been cautioned and repeats the offence later in the match, he must be sent off. If a referee forces a wall to retreat ten yards at one end, he must not allow it to encroach to within eight yards at the other.

Commonsense A referee is faced with all sorts of problems coming at him from every direction. He must be able to apply commonsense. Sort out what is right and what is wrong, what requires action and what does not. Don't use a rebuking shout, when a quiet word will do. Never over-react. A missile might be thrown by a spectator. I am certainly not condoning that type of behaviour, but the player closest to where the projectile lands could exaggerate the incident out of all proportion. He might want me to stop the game or even lead the players off – always the last resort. A good policy here is to look at or consult a policeman, who has probably seen the missile land. The man from the law will be objective about the seriousness of the offence.

However, referee George Courtney had no alternative but to lead the players back to the dressing rooms when fans invaded the pitch for the second time during the Birmingham v West Ham FA Cup fifth round tie in February 1984. This was the first match which the refereeing team from England for the 1984 European Championships of Courtney (referee), myself (senior linesman) and Keith Miller (other linesman) had had together, and it was ironic we should be confronted by such a major problem as we attempted to familiarise ourselves with each other's style.

The match was virtually safe for Birmingham. They were 2-0 in front and had been awarded a penalty. A number of spectators climbed on to the fence surrounding the pitch but the police, present in force, were able to prevent them from getting on to the pitch. Birmingham duly went three goals ahead and that, for the time being, was the end of the matter.

Sometime later, shouts of, 'We want to stop the game!' began coming from the crowd. The police, aware of the pending danger, congregated around the fenced-off (terraced) area of the ground where, normally, the principal trouble comes from. Surprisingly, though, a number of people from the seated areas of the ground ran onto the pitch. The invasion seemed more mischievous – a dare, if you like – than violent. I ran towards the referee because I think it is important to have a double view of the incident and be able to discuss any action that might be taken. We spoke to the chief of police, allowed the situation to calm down and the game re-commenced.

But shortly afterwards there was another surge. This time it was bigger. It started with fans from the seats and then they started spilling over the fences as well. Soon, there were pitched battles. The referee was pushed firmly in the back, we consulted and George made in my view, the wise decision to lead the players off the pitch. The players were at risk, no doubt about that. Billy Bonds, the buccaneering West Ham captain, had run off the pitch and was attempting to stop West Ham fans coming onto the field. He was actually turning some of them back. I never recommend that players get involved with spectators, because they leave themselves open to danger. One day a player might be beaten up on the pitch. But Bonds' intentions were thoroughly admirable and it was clear that the players themselves abhorred yet another demonstration of hooliganism. I went back to the dressing room thinking, 'What next?' When I was a youngster, I never dreamed we would see the day when there was pitch perimeter fencing – cages – at football grounds. Soon many pitches will surely be completely surrounded by fencing. What comes after that? Moats? England, a country noted for its sportsmanship and fair play, has an atrocious reputation abroad for football spectator violence. I know because I have been there and heard many people talking about it. Sometimes, it makes me ashamed.

Any official, indeed anybody connected with football, must be concerned about the hooligan problem. It seems to me that so many people do not respect the police and authority in the way they used to and the way I was always brought up to. When I am driving and notice a police car in my rear view mirror, my heart rate goes up a little. I wonder if I am doing something wrong. The same respect should be felt towards the law by people watching football matches.

There is a Yorkshire saying, 'They pay their money, they are allowed to shout.' Quite right too. But a minority go over the top. There are so many contributory factors – drunkenness, inadequate punishments, under-policing, lack of parental discipline and so on. My major concern is the safety of the players and, when things such as coins and bottles are thrown from the crowd, their lives are put at risk in the sense that although they will probably not be killed, they could lose their livelihood. A player, travelling at speed down the wing and struck in the face by an object thrown from the crowd, might never play football again.

But it is important not to become too dramatic. Put it all in perspective. A month before that Birmingham v West Ham Cup tie, I refereed a game between Luton and Arsenal at Kenilworth Road. After just three or four minutes play, a section of the crowd surged onto the pitch. I had to make a decision. Should I call a halt to the match completely or attempt to play it down? I take the view that, whenever possible, I should play it down. On this occasion, the ball had gone for a throw-in close to where I was standing. I shouted to the thrower, 'Hold on to the ball!' The ground stewards and police reacted very quickly and were able to disperse the crowd. Whether or not it was a deliberate invasion or just a swell of the crowd was of no immediate concern to me. All I cared about was that people were on the pitch. In this particular instance, the problem quickly disappeared and I would like to think that I helped by applying a little bit of commonsense and not over-reacting.

I thought referee Tony Morrisey was demonstrating a good deal of commonsense when the Wolves teamsheet had still not arrived in our dressing room by 2.33 p.m. before their match at Newcastle a few years ago. The rules stipulate that they must be in no later than thirty minutes before kick-off, but we knew that the Wolves' coach had been delayed and that their arrival at St James's Park was imminent. There was no danger of the match itself being delayed. Suddenly, the Wolves manager came dashing into our room with his teamsheet. Morrisey said, 'I'm sure you realise that you're three minutes late. I know the reason, but try not to let it happen again.' I was the linesman and I thought Tony's attitude was just right. He could have reported Wolves to the Football League and caused them considerable problems.

Suddenly, a chap from the television company who were covering the match knocked on the door, walked in and said, 'What's the fine for late arrival of teamsheets?'

'What?' came Tony's stunned reply.

'We've just gone out on TV and told the world that the Wolves teamsheet was late.'

Tony then had to go somewhat sheepishly into the Wolves' dressing room and inform them that they would be reported for submitting their teamsheet late.

Another area that requires commonsense is when players attempt to get other players into trouble. I despise this type of behaviour. A player who claims he has been fouled and wants to lie down and die, shouting that his alleged assailant should be sent-off, will find no smypathy with me, but it is important not to allow scepticism to blind you to a genuine case.

But faking – which in my book is cheating – happens all the time. Players frequently feign that they have been clipped from behind when there was no contact, in an attempt to get a free kick, and it is not just forwards who are guilty of this fraud. But when forwards are within the vicinity of the penalty area, the amount of diving increases. The referee must use his commonsense to sort out the fake from the real thing.

I have never been more grateful to a policeman for getting me out of a difficult position than when I was invited to referee a match between Sheffield Wednesday and the Nigerian national team at Hillsborough. The game had been tough, with a number of players being cautioned. I awarded a free kick to Wednesday when a Nigerian player casually walked up to Gary Megson, the Wednesday midfield player, and poleaxed him with a right-hand punch. I saw the incident and immediately produced the red card. Suddenly, though, the offender was surrounded by his team-mates and, in the thick of the action, all these Nigerian players looked the same. Although, in the back of my mind, I was sure that the number six was the offender. I moved away from the melee of players, still holding the red card aloft and pointing to the tunnel. 'I can't stand here all day holding this red card in the air,' I thought. 'One of them has got to go soon or otherwise I'm going to look a right fool.'

Then, perhaps with a mixture of inspiration and commonsense, I beckoned one of the policemen by the touchline on to the pitch. I do not think I have ever seen a player disappear more rapidly down the tunnel than the Nigerian number six!

8

The Players

One of the greatest joys of refereeing Football League matches is that I am able to watch outstanding players from closer quarters than any spectators. Somebody can buy a ticket for the most expensive seat in the ground, but his view of the action will never compare with mine. From this short range, I can truly appreciate the ability of many of the men who make their living from playing the sport. All referees are football lovers. Although our view of each match is objective and impartial, we are in many ways like the fellow on the terraces. We admire a magnificent goal or piece of skill. The only difference is that we do not show it.

The referee's principal task is to allow the players to express their talent to the paying public. To help make the match a spectacle that will satisfy the customers. The referee, therefore, should attempt to blend into the background as much as possible, giving the players a largely free hand. A platform on which to display their ability. Sometimes, though, the actions of even the greatest players necessitate intervention from the official.

They do not come much greater than Kenny Dalglish, the only man to score a century of goals in both Scottish and Football League matches. I have refereed Liverpool more than most since Kenny's transfer from Celtic in August 1977. Week in, week out, his consistently high level of skill is remarkable and, for the past few years, he has been the singular most influential player in British soccer. From a referee's point of view, though, Kenny can be a difficult player to control. He will put his arm and his rear anywhere in an effort to get the ball and I know that at times, he is guilty of backing into his defender and then, when he finishes on the ground, appealing for a free kick, when in fact he is the one who has perpetrated the foul. But I also think that there are times when he is genuinely flattened by a defender and he does not receive the necessary protection.

Referees sometimes do not read him properly. In not one of the matches in which I have handled Liverpool has Kenny disputed one of my decisions so strongly that I have had to issue a caution. With Ian Rush possessing the speed to run on to so many of Dalglish's defence-bisecting passes and the skill to accept a high proportion of the opportunities his speed helps create, Liverpool are an awesome prospect when moving forward.

A lot of people have compared Rush to Jimmy Greaves and there is no doubt that Liverpool's Welsh striker possesses superb positional sense and clinical finishing. But, to me, he is more like Bobby Charlton. This is because, like Charlton, he has the ability to shoot at goal from distance whereas Greaves was almost exclusively a 'poacher' of goals from close range.

Liverpool are not so bad at the back, either. Phil Neal, their international right back, is a man with whom I have had a number of exchanges – invariably agreeable – and I admire his responsible attitude. I refereed the first 'live' FA Cup tie (apart from the Final itself) to be shown on British television. Liverpool beat Newcastle 4-0 in the third round in January 1984 and, during the course of the game, Phil was struck on the head by a coin or similar object thrown from the crowd. He made so little fuss that many people did not even notice he had been hit. Phil simply walked to the touchline to receive treatment for the wound and then carried on with the game. I am sure his sensible actions prevented trouble flaring during the match – and the fact that there were crowd disturbances after the game was for an altogether different reason. Phil Neal might have received more criticism than most internationals in his time, but I have always been able to understand why England selected him so frequently. He always seems to have so much time – a sure sign of a class player – and 'reads' the game magnificently. Quite apart from his defensive qualities, a delicate pass or long run down the wing from Neal has put Liverpool on the offensive on so many occasions.

Graeme Souness, the former Liverpool captain who went to Sampdoria in the Italian League, is a midfield player who combines both combative and creative qualities in his game. One game involving Souness that stands out was an FA Cup tie between Blackburn Rovers and Liverpool in January 1983. In the opening minutes, Souness committed a late foul tackle on Blackburn's Noel Brotherston. I awarded a free kick and informed Souness that I was going to caution him. His reply was, 'You were at the top of my list of referees, but now you're at the bottom.'

'You are going to be at the top of my list of players right here in the book,' was my retort as I took his name, 'and if you repeat that type of foul again, I will have no alternative but to send you off.'

Souness most certainly did not find that amusing. My little quip, designed to ease the tension, backfired. I must add, though, that Souness, whose determination to succeed and whose unstinting effort in every game were so beneficial to Liverpool, behaved impeccably for the remainder of the match.

Emlyn 'Crazy Horse' Hughes became a legendary figure on Merseyside. His enthusiasm was infectious and my first confrontation with him was after only three minutes of my initial match at Anfield – Liverpool versus West Bromwich Albion in August 1977. Kenny Dalglish was brought down very close to the edge of the Albion penalty area. I immediately looked at my linesman, who confirmed the offence had taken place outside the box. As I was supervising the free kick, I could hear one or two Liverpool players muttering amongst themselves that a penalty should have been awarded. Suddenly, Emlyn ran up to me, protesting vehemently that I had made a mistake and should have given a penalty. He was several yards behind where the foul took place and clearly in no position to judge, and his ranting and raving was so strong that I informed Emlyn that I was going to caution him.

'Could I please have your name?' I asked the man who, at the time, was captain of both Liverpool and England.

'You know it,' came his curt reply.

I eventually persuaded him to spell out his name and then he turned and shouted towards his own team-mates, 'You'd better keep quiet when this ref is about. You can't even talk to him without being booked.'

I had no further problems, either in that match or any other in which I handled him – and those included a number of important matches. Emlyn was an outstanding leader and motivator of men and he always played the game with a smile. If one of the younger Liverpool players threatened to step out of line, Emlyn would do his best to make sure the youngster kept out of trouble. Football must be an abiding passion for Emlyn. I recall once bumping into him at Southport, on a cold mid-winter evening, apparently there for no other reason than to watch the game. As usual, Emlyn wore a smile and welcomed me with a greeting of, 'Hi, ref!'

The King of the Kop during the seventies was Kevin Keegan. I handled matches involving him on a number of occasions after his return to English football following his spell in the West German Bundesliga with SV Hamburg, during which he was twice voted European Footballer of the Year. He has done a tremendous amount for the game. People always talk about Keegan's workrate, but they often disregard his skill which, although not in the same class as somebody like George Best, was still considerable. But I think the single most amazing aspect of Keegan's game was his ability to gain phenomenal height from his relatively short frame, when going up for headers.

Keegan earned a lot of money out of the game, and I think earned is the operative word. It was a pity he decided to retire at the end of the 1983-84 season. Football needs players of his calibre and characters of his stature. But you have to admire somebody who calls it a day when still at the top. Keegan would rarely speak when he wanted to dispute a decision. He would look. If he thought the referee had made a mistake, he made his feelings known with a facial expression or an accusing glance. Perhaps that is the best way, because it almost certainly avoids confrontation with referees.

Keegan played first for Southampton on his return from Germany and then became the hero of the football-crazy Geordies at St James's Park. He met up at Newcastle with his former Liverpool colleague, Terry McDermott, who in 1980 was elected both the Football Writers' Footballer of the Year and the PFA Player of the Year, at the time a unique double honour. But McDermott was a player who never impressed me. He won those two awards in a superb Liverpool team, of which he was an integral part, but I always thought there were other players who were equally, if not more, effective.

Behind the Liverpool defence for the past few seasons has been the extrovert Bruce Grobbelaar, the master of the unexpected, but also a superbly-conditioned athlete – flexible and with lightning reflexes. Bruce's predecessor, before he moved south to Tottenham, was Ray Clemence. I have been refereeing Liverpool games, and the Red's pressure has been so intense and concentrated, that Clemence has scarcely touched the ball for several minutes. Suddenly, though, the opposition would escape the siege and mount a rare assault of their own. This is when Clemence is superb – he has the ability to produce an important save when virtually 'cold'.

For years, Clemence vied for the England number one shirt with Peter Shilton, a man whose desire to be the greatest goalkeeper in the world borders on obsession. When refereeing Nottingham Forest and later Southampton, I always kept an eye on Shilton. One of his idiosyncrasies is that he likes to dig a groove in the penalty area, to act as a guide to the whereabouts of his posts and the centre of the goal. This, of course, is illegal and is a cautionable offence.

I always found Southampton, under the charge of Lawrie McMenemy, an interesting lot. On the one hand, there was the skill of players such as

Danny Wallace, the fast and talented winger, and Frank Worthington, who has so many deft touches. Nomadic Frank went to another south coast club, Brighton, after leaving the Dell. Then there were the more abrasive qualities of Steve Williams, the team's captain before leaving for Arsenal. Williams is a highly-gifted player, but unfortunately there have been times when he wanted to argue with virtually every decision given by a referee. When I handled Southampton with Williams in the side, it is no exaggeration to say that I would have been quite justified in cautioning him for dissent in something like the third minute of many games, and I have taken his name on more than one occasion.

I am not sure if this argumentative nature is just excessive enthusiasm or a deliberate ploy to attempt to put me off my game, but I can assure him it would never succeed, because I am quite used to players exerting this kind of pressure. Williams is not a player one needs to keep an eye on solely because of his comments to the officials. He is also a hard tackler and, sometimes, his keenness to win the ball becomes too vigorous and over-physical, perhaps even cynical. He has been selected for England, which is an interesting choice, but he must be warned. He is going to have to learn that comments and animated disagreements will land him in trouble with referees in the international arena. If Williams starts throwing his arms about or spouting a torrent of dissent when disputing a referee's decision, he is showing to everybody that he is questioning the official's verdict and will receive very short shrift from referees. Officials from abroad are not always renowned for their tolerance and Williams' name is almost bound to go instantly into the book. It would be a tragedy if Williams' character prevented him becoming an established England international, because the man has skill in abundance. He must learn to win the ball with his hard tackles, but legitimately, and keep his mouth shut.

Mick Mills, who made a record 591 League appearances for Ipswich before moving to The Dell, is another difficult player. He always wants to argue with the referee, to get his twopenceworth. A typical chain of events might be that Mills commits a foul and then attempts to 'disappear'. I would say, 'Hey, Millsey, just calm down!' And he would retort with an outburst.

A Southampton player I have had the highest regard for – both on and off the field – is David Armstrong, whose durability and desire to shake off bumps and bruises means he hardly ever misses a match. I have refereed David many times, both when he was at Middlesbrough and later with the Saints. He has plenty of skill and energy and I have always found him a tremendous help during a match. If one of his team-mates is getting a little out of hand and needs a quiet speaking to, I can normally get a word through to David, who will have the necessary chat with his colleague. As a player, David is highly underrated. He can be attacking one minute and kicking balls off his own line the next.

I remember being invited, along with Neil Midgley, to a Southern League Referees' Association meeting at Bournemouth. David Armstrong was there and we spent an informative and enjoyable weekend together. David was able to pass on useful and interesting information to referees.

Apart from Shilton and Clemence, the Football League has certainly been blessed with a plethora of other outstanding goalkeepers in recent years. Joe Corrigan would have been an automatic choice for most other countries but, with the presence of Clemence and Shilton, made only a handful of England appearances. I particularly remember Joe's magnificent performance in the first match of the Centenary FA Cup Final, when he was deservedly voted Man of the Match.

The grand old man of goalkeepers for several years, though, has been the incomparable Pat Jennings. Few more respected characters can have played the game and he also has a marvellous rapport, even with the opposition fans. He is universally admired. I have refereed Pat on a number of occasions and in some very important games. His demeanour has never been anything other than honest and likeable. I cannot recall him disputing one of my decisions and some of his saves simply take the breath away.

After refereeing the FA Cup semi-final first replay between Arsenal and Liverpool at Villa Park in 1980 – I had also done the first match at Hillsborough – I remember walking out of the ground and bumping into Pat. He said, 'See you for the next match. We're all enjoying ourselves.' When I told him that I would not be refereeing the third game, because the referee had been changed, there was a look of genuine disappointment on his face. I felt a great sense of pride. Jennings, already the first British professional footballer to play more than 1000 first-class games, is in good enough physical shape to continue playing for a year or two yet. It was sad to hear of his 'official' retirement at the end of the 1984-85 season.

Another one of Arsenal's outstanding Irish footballers is Republic international David O'Leary, considered by many one of the finest centre backs in Europe. I remember the 1983 FA Cup semi-final between Arsenal and Manchester United, which United won and then went on to beat Brighton at Wembley after a replay. The semi-final was at Villa Park and, during the game, O'Leary committed a foul which was immediately followed by a retaliatory foul by a United player. I had already blown for the O'Leary foul. I supervised the placing of the ball, ran to my position and blew for the kick to be taken. Next day, I was astonished to be asked by several people why I had allowed O'Leary to call me a cheat. I watched the video recording of the game and I must admit it does look as though that is what David says to me. In a quarter of a century of refereeing, I have never once cheated, and any player who accused me of so doing would be dismissed instantly from the field. I either did not hear O'Leary call me a cheat or he said something similar that, to amateur lip-readers, looked the same.

The roving eye of the television camera often notices things that players and referees do not spot. The referee might make a decision and leave the scene as soon as possible to avoid any confrontation, while the cameras linger, recording comments and actions, not always complimentary towards the referee, for an audience of millions.

Brian Talbot of Arsenal can be aggressive. Not necessarily in the malicious sense, but because his determination and enthusiasm occasionally spill over. Few players cover more ground during the course of a game. He is an absolute machine and runs his heart out. He is all over the place and, if the referee is not careful, he can bump into Talbot if he is running an opposite diagonal. When handling Arsenal, I can often hear Talbot shouting, 'Hey, ref, get out the way! Get out of the way!'

I met Charlie Nicholas in my first international match – Scotland against Northern Ireland in 1983 – which finished goalless. It was a game that rarely touched the heights, but Nicholas's contribution was useful. The next time I handled Nicholas was when he was playing for Arsenal at Luton in January 1984. He fired shots over the crossbar on two or three occasions and I could sense the pressure on him. He had been the goalscoring sensation for Celtic in the Scottish League, cost Arsenal £750,000 and was expected to produce a similar goal blitz when he came south. But there were times when it did not happen. The coaching in England is tight and players do not have as many opportunities to strike at goal as in Scotland.

Arsenal have not been so successful since the departure of those two outstanding Republic of Ireland internationals, Liam Brady and Frank Stapleton. Brady, lured by the lira, extended his career in Italy, but not before I had watched him play from the middle. I recall refereeing a game between Liverpool and Arsenal at Anfield. Brady had the ball and wriggled past one challenge, past two, past three and then shot narrowly over the bar. The first attempted tackle warranted a free kick in Brady's favour, but I decided to allow play to run. I was pleased I did not stop the game, because it would have robbed the crowd of a marvellous piece of skill and Brady of a goalscoring opportunity. I thought, 'Crikey, what a superbly skilful player.' Brady's talents incorporated accurate long and short passing, a telling shot, marvellous vision and deceptive strength. People accused him of being unduly left-footed, but what a left foot. And it would not be true to say that he used his right leg purely for standing on. I have seen him deliver plenty with his right boot.

Stapleton is cast in the mould of the old-fashioned centre forward, strong and dominating in the air. But that does not mean that he lacks skill, and he also puts in a tremendous amount of work outside the penalty area. Like many strikers, Stapleton is not averse to making a challenge look worse that it really is when he senses he is not going to reach the ball, especially when inside the eighteen-yard area.

Stapleton succeeded Joe Jordan as Manchester United's main strike weapon. Joe, who went from United, via Italy, to Southampton, is a hard player and is certainly not afraid to throw his weight around – although, I must admit that I have never had too much trouble from him. But from what other referees tell me, and from what I have seen on television, Joe's aggression has been known to exceed legal limits.

Gordon McQueen, of Manchester United and Scotland, is another outstanding central defender and rightly renowned for his aerial power, both in defence and at attacking set pieces, but the greatest thrill he has given to the Old Trafford spectators is when charging downfield, kamikaze fashion, with the ball at his feet. It entertains the crowd and also presents problems to opponents.

Bryan Robson and Ray Wilkins, the latter a player who can pass with pinpoint accuracy and another to try his hand in Italy, present no problems to a referee. Their total commitment is to the game and I think they keep their concentration on that and not on what the referee is doing. Robson, the captain of Manchester United and England, has a responsible attitude and will often talk to one of his colleagues, clearly advising him to calm down. Alternatively, he might come to the defence of a player with a comment such as, 'Hey ref, it's only a bit of youthful enthusiasm.' Some players are particularly prone to do this, especially experienced campaigners in the lower divisions who have spent the bulk of their careers in the First Division and are keen to protect a raw youngster who might just be emerging in a club's first team.

If Manchester United, Spurs and Everton currently pose the greatest threat to Liverpool's dominance of the domestic game, there is no doubt that in the late seventies and early eighties, Nottingham Forest, under Brian Clough and Peter Taylor, were the team Liverpool watched with greatest trepidation.

Larry Lloyd, the former Forest centre half who also played for Liverpool and then entered the management merry-go-round, is a player who springs to mind when I think of Forest. I was invited to referee a friendly match between Forest and Tampa Bay Rowdies at the City Ground, which, to the delight of everyone, attracted 18,000 spectators – many of them in family groups. Before the start, Brian Clough mentioned to me that, if any member of his team was giving problems, I should nod in his direction and he would take the necessary action. In the opening minutes, Lloyd disputed a couple of my decisions and was letting his mouth run away from him. It looked as though the only way I would quieten him down would be to take his name, but before I could remove my notebook from my pocket, the Forest substitute stripped off ready to come on. The large card indicating the number of the player to be substituted was shown and Lloyd was the man Clough brought off. It certainly avoided any further problems.

John McGovern and Ian Bowyer were generals in midfield for Forest, players who seemed to keep things ticking over. Another man in midfield was Archie Gemmill, a player with whom I have clashed quite often, both in Football League matches and in the North American Soccer League. Archie is dynamic, tenacious and fiercely committed. His level of effort is amazing and he becomes totally engrossed in each game, getting stuck in and being vociferous. Throughout the match, I can always hear Archie hurling advice to his team-mates, especially if they are failing to respond to his demands.

Over the years, John Robertson has been a delight to watch. Skilful, tormenting almost, he shows a defender just enough of the ball to coax a lunge. In effect, he is saying, 'Here it is, come and get it.' Robertson would then, usually successfully, skip past the defender's desperate tackle and send over a telling cross for the likes of Garry Birtles or Peter Withe.

I once had a run of taking Peter Withe's name. Every time he was in a match I was handling, I seemed to end up cautioning Withe, almost without exception for dissent. Withe always attempts to dominate his opponents and his desire to win often leads to frustration, with unacceptably fierce disagreement with my decision and a caution the outcome. I have learned to keep my distance from Withe because I know he wants to dispute anything and everything and argue about whatever does not meet with his total approval.

Withe subsequently moved to Newcastle and then Aston Villa, where he played an important part in their League Championship triumph in 1981. (He has since joined Sheffield United.) That Villa side was captained by Dennis Mortimer, a strong-tackling player and a man who, to my surprise, never played for England. There are a number of good club players who have never received international recognition. Mortimer needs to be a dominant skipper, because Villa are a side with several strong personalities, each of whom would probably captain the side if at another club.

Tottenham started the influx of South American players, which has dried up a little recently, when they signed Argentinians Osvaldo Ardiles and Ricardo Villa shortly after the 1978 World Cup finals. The referee had to realise that the Latin temperament was different from that of the typical English player and make a few allowances. Ardiles wanted to argue with every decision when he first came to England. It would have been easy to caution him for dissent, but I preferred to show a vestige of tolerance and hope he would lose this argumentative side to his game as he became familiar with the English style. And he did. There were a few problems of communication with the Argentinians – Villa's English, particularly, was virtually non-existent to begin with – but gestures with the arms and expressions with the face form a universal language.

Villa is a player whose deeds I will never forget. His goal that won the Centenary FA Cup Final for Spurs against Manchester City, when he beat three or four defenders, was one of the finest I have ever seen. And Villa, who had been substituted in the first instalment of the Final, could not have chosen a more dramatic stage.

Graham Roberts is one of the hardest players in the Spurs side, indeed in the entire First Division. He is constantly backwards and forwards and usually finishes the game with the dirtiest shirt. Then there is the finesse of Glenn Hoddle, who is similar in style to Tony Currie, the former Sheffield United, Leeds and Queen's Park Rangers midfield player. People often complain that players such as Hoddle and Currie do not work hard enough on the pitch, but I have seen them both sweating like pigs. Because they have plenty of time and often stop, look up and actually think what they are going to do with the ball before they kick it, people accuse them of laziness. Hoddle and Currie do most things on the football field with such consummate ease.

Andy Gray, back again with Aston Villa after moving to Wolves and Everton, has a justified reputation for total commitment. He is quite prepared to put his head among the flying boots if it might lead to a goalscoring opportunity. Andy has never been a problem to me and I have seen him have some superb games. If he has a shot at goal or a decent header, Gray is the sort of player to whom I can say something like, 'Hey, that wasn't bad.' On the other hand, Gray might push a player or commit a foul and my remark might be, 'I saw that. Now cut it out because I want to keep the game flowing.' Either way, Gray responds in the right way. These small snippets of conversation can ease the tension and help the referee acquire the respect of the players. I would like to think that Gray respects my refereeing and I know I enjoy officiating players of his type – hard, maybe, but knowing where to draw the line.

Adrian Heath, Gray's colleague in the Everton team that started to emerge from Liverpool's red shadow by reaching both the Milk Cup and FA Cup Finals in 1983, is a skilful and knowledgeable player. But he is another who at times wants to argue with the referee, which I think is a pity because it takes his concentration away from his game, and I am sure that it does not improve his performance. Heath is a small man, around five foot six, and men of such stature often feel they need to compensate for their lack of inches by showing more aggression. They also believe that they should receive more protection from the referee. Peter Reid is another Everton player who has a profound influence on the side.

Ipswich, under Bobby Robson, were one of the top sides in the country for a decade. Yet, they did not win much in the way of trophies to show for it. Their players, apart from perhaps Mick Mills when he was at Portman Road, gave me few problems. A number of them have moved on now, but for a long time Ipswich had a settled side. John Wark, Eric Gates, Alan Brazil and Paul Mariner are the type of players who get on with and seem to enjoy the game. You can smile at them. Frans Thijssen, who joined Nottingham Forest after leaving Ipswich, and Arnold Muhren, who went to Manchester United, arrived from the Dutch club Twente Enschede and their sharply-honed skills were important to Ipswich. Thijssen and Muhren also spoke fluent English, so communication was never a problem. If either of them was suddenly to launch a verbal attack on me in Dutch, I do not think I would need to be a master of perception to understand what they meant. I suspect it is unlikely they were telling me that the nine o'clock bus was not leaving the station until twenty past! Paul Cooper, the Ipswich goalkeeper, I have always found quiet in his approach; he goes about his business in a thoroughly professional manner. I admire that.

West Ham are not a team whose players generally cause trouble, and nobody set a better example than Trevor Brooking, the elegant ambassador who, like Keegan, retired at the end of the 1983-84 season. Trevor has the ability to win himself so much time with the ball, enabling him to distribute telling passes, and he was deceptively difficult to shake off the ball. Billy Bonds, who has played more games for the club than any other player, lost none of his enthusiasm over the years. Phil Parkes, yet another outstanding English goalkeeper of the modern generation, is a major influence behind the back four and Alan Devonshire, who has never seemed to recapture his club form when he played for England, can bewilder opponents with his speed and skill. It would be a shame if injury ruined his career. I have always liked refereeing West Ham and I remember the second leg of the semi-final of the 1981 League Cup against Coventry, which was a thrilling match. The action was incessant and it was the type of game that can only be good for football. West Ham won the game at Upton Park 2-0 and progressed to the Final against Liverpool by an aggregate of 4-3.

I remember going into a bookshop a few years ago and picking up a book and flicking through the pages. There were several good action photographs and I was determining whether to buy it. Suddenly, the book opened at a picture of John Wile, Kenny Dalglish and myself. It was taken during my first match at Anfield, between Liverpool and West Bromwich Albion. Wile was holding Dalglish's shirt out of my vision and I was looking at the two players. I came across Wile during my summer in the States and also since his entry into management with Peterborough United. He was a linchpin of the Albion side for a decade and was the archetypal good, honest, hard professional. Uncompromising, but nothing dirty.

Albion, under a variety of managers, have had a series of excellent players in recent years, yet somehow have never quite fulfilled their potential. Bryan Robson, Remi Moses, Laurie Cunningham, Cyrille Regis, Garry Thompson, Derek Statham, Ally Robertson, Ally Brown, Martyn Bennett and Brendon Batson are just some of the talented individuals who have been at The Hawthorns, but the club has little to show for it. I was certainly disappointed with West Brom when I did their 1982 FA Cup semi-final against Queen's Park Rangers. The team simply never got going.

Some might say that Regis, a strong fit player, with all the necessary physical equipment to be an outstanding international player, somehow typified Albion before he joined Coventry. He has not really done himself justice, although a number of injuries have not helped his progress. Regis has not had a decent run in the England team. Indeed, I often wonder whether we give our international players the opportunity to establish themselves and perform to the full extent of their ability at that level. They might make a mistake, or have a mediocre game, and they are out of the side. Perhaps a player should be guaranteed four or five games. It might take him that long before he has the confidence to attempt the type of thing he is doing without a second thought for his club. If I appoint a salesman, I do not expect him to be a top-liner the next day. I expect him to be managed, encouraged and taught until he eventually does the job effectively, and it should be the same with the England football team. That is where countries like Northern Ireland and Wales do so well. They do not have the same resources as England to select from, yet they have a more settled nucleus to the side. So somebody such as Noel Brotherston, the Blackburn midfield player, has become a highly effective performer at international level.

Queen's Park Rangers, who won that 1982 semi-final before losing to Tottenham in the Final at Wembley, are a team containing some interesting characters. Bob Hazell's confrontation with Regis that day was full-blooded to say the least. Both are exceptionally powerful players and the earth was shaken. Other powerful black men include Noel Blake who joined Portsmouth from Birmingham, and George Berry, of Wolves and later Stoke. They contrast with the more silken skills of blacks such as Danny Wallace and John Chiedozie, who must be the fastest man in the First Division. Especially when they first appeared regularly in the Football League, the black players needed man-managing carefully, sometimes by helping them ignore the 'stick' they were receiving from certain sections of the crowd.

Returning to Rangers, I recall seeing their player, Simon Stainrod, now with Aston Villa, on television when he was involved in a clash with Manchester United's Gordon McQueen in literally the first minute. It might have been six of one and half a dozen of the other, and an obvious attempt to 'soften each other up' for the rest of the game. But it did make me wonder quite how necessary the collision was. It set a discouraging precedent for the match and might have been the start of a running feud. Stainrod is a player who has plenty of ability, but at times he does appear to do his best to squander or misdirect it. I remember another occasion, also against United, when he pushed a Manchester United player into the penalty area and claimed encroachment when United scored with the kick.

Rangers' Omniturf pitch has also been the subject of much interest. I believe I am in some position to pass judgement, having refereed many games on synthetic surfaces during my eight weeks operating in the North American Soccer League during the summer of 1982. I have also handled games at Loftus Road. I encountered a number of different artificial surfaces in America – some good, some bad, some indifferent. Certainly the plastic pitch at New York's Giants' Stadium was excellent. The bounce was authentic, the run clean and the surface possessed characteristics similar to those of grass. Nobody could claim that was the case at Loftus Road, where the bounce and pace were both excessive when the pitch was first laid. When Rangers sprinkled around 250 tons of sand on the pitch for the start of the 1984-85 season though, the result was an enormous improvement in the way the pitch played.

Visiting players – and referees – needed to adjust very quickly when playing on Rangers' Omniturf in its first few seasons. As the ball bounced to a greater height, consequently spending more time in the air, the official needed to keep a particular eye on the players. A player might position himself to head the ball as he would on a grass surface but, as the extra bounce meant the ball took longer to arrive, he might be out of position when it did. He might have used his arms illegally in frustration. Rangers are more experienced than other teams on their pitch, and, therefore, normal advantage cannot always be played. What might be advantageous to a side on grass, could land them in peril on the carpet, because a player is not able to control or reach the fast-moving ball.

I must admit that I am a traditionalist and maintain that soccer is a game for grass, but if more of these synthetic surfaces are to infiltrate into our game, they must be utilised to the full. A stadium, when near a high conurbation area, has a high cost factor that is rising and not reducing. Therefore, the stadium must be put to multi-use. The one at Seattle, which holds between thirty and forty thousand spectators and has a plastic pitch, is rarely inactive. Almost immediately after I refereed Seattle Sounders against San Jose Earthquakes, several tons of dirt were tipped onto the pitch and, the following day, the stadium was the scene of a motor-cycle racing competition. Although Rangers have never had to postpone a match on their pitch, I am not sure they utilise it to the full. It would be the ideal setting, for example, for a pop concert, although I understand that protests from the local residents have prompted the council to block Rangers' proposals for one or two pop concerts.

While in America, incidentally, I came across several Football League players. Steve Hunt, who almost seems to commute between England and the States, has been an outstanding player in the NASL for New York Cosmos, showing speed, the ability to take on opposing players and finishing power. Yet he never truly reproduced that type of form for Coventry and West Brom.

Steve Daley, who cost almost £1,500,000 when transferred from Wolves to Manchester City but then failed to achieve a great deal at Maine Road, is another star in the States. He has scored a stack of goals for Seattle Sounders. Vince Hilaire of Crystal Palace, now with Portsmouth, also excited the crowd when I saw him play in America and Gordon Hill, the former England international left-winger, is another favourite with the fans over there.

Also while in America, I certainly had my fair share of contretemps with that Italian forward, Giorgio Chinaglia. Apart from Chinaglia's fight with Caesar Romero, his own New York Cosmos team-mate, at the end of the game against Chicago – described elsewhere – I was also involved in a heated discussion of sorts with him during Cosmos' match against Vancouver Whitecaps. Soon after the start, Chinaglia put the ball into the net, but I disallowed the effort because he had clearly pushed a defender. Chingalia ran towards me with a torrent of dissent so strong that I had no option but to pluck a yellow card from my pocket.

He was amazed and said, 'Do you know who I am?'

'No. So could you please give me your name?'

With Chinaglia not at his most helpful and my Italian at best pidgin, an inordinate amount of time elapsed before I finally wrote his name – spelt correctly – in my notebook.

Hill, who made his England appearances during his days at Manchester United and subsequently played for Derby and Queen's Park Rangers, seemed to fade quickly out of the English game. I remember refereeing United against Sunderland and Hill, after arguing strongly with one of my linesmen – which, in effect, is the same as arguing with the referee – went straight into the notebook in the opening minutes. He tended to start a dialogue with officials. Hill, on the left, and right-winger Steve Coppell formed a highly exciting and dangerous two-pronged assault down the flanks for Manchester United during the time that Tommy Docherty was manager. While Hill moved on, Coppell remained until he was tragically forced to give up the game at the age of twenty-eight because of a recurring knee injury. Coppell was a tremendous player and I am sure both England and United miss him more than, perhaps, they realised they would. He could be an out-and-out winger, with speed and skill, or occupy a more defensive role on the right side of midfield. Just occasionally, Coppell would become frustrated, blow a valve and over-react. But I never had any real problems with him.

I remember giving a lecture to a meeting in Coventry in which we were talking abut the 'professional foul'. Coppell was there in his role as chairman of the Professional Footballers Association. I ended my talk with a series of video shots of horrendous tackles with a voice-over along the lines of, 'And this is just the sort of thing we are trying to eliminate.' One of the fouls was committed by Coppell, who was sitting impassively at the back of the room. It could not have been better (or worse) timed. But Steve took it in the right spirit and we all had a good laugh. Coppell was a player to whom I could play a high level of advantage; I knew he would continue with the ball and not stop and have a go at the player who had just fouled him. If all players accepted advantage in this way, referees would be able to slip into the background much more during a match and keep the game flowing to a greater extent.

Coppell, who became manager of Crystal Palace, combined football with taking a degree in Economics at Liverpool University during the early part of his career. He is not the only person to split soccer with studies. Steve Heighway and Alan Gowling are two others. These are men who have not spent all their working life training every day with a club and, as a result, they have sometimes seemed 'fresher' on match day. Perhaps there is a lesson there. Gowling, incidentally, is a marvellous example to other players. His attitude has always been, 'I'll deal with that, ref. I'll sort it out.' And, being so articulate, he is better able to communicate than most players.

Every player in the Football League has certain qualities, but some have caught my eye more than others. And they are not necessarily international stars or household names. I think of Glenn Roeder and David McCreery, who came together at Newcastle, but who were players probably best remembered for spells at Queen's Park Rangers and Manchester United respectively – Roeder for his speed and skill when moving clear of defence (not least his 'double shuffle' in which he passes his foot over the ball) and McCreery for his sheer stamina. Mickey Thomas and Sammy McIlroy, who have both played for Stoke and Manchester United, have each got plenty of tricks in their repertoire, and Mark Wallington, the Leicester goalkeeper who has captained the side, has a responsible attitude and I have seen him make some superb saves.

Chris Woods, the Norwich goalkeeper who began his career under Brian Clough at Nottingham Forest and found himself in a League Cup Final against Liverpool at Wembley before his career had scarcely begun, is probably the best of the generation likely to take over from Shilton and Clemence. And Dave Watson, capped sixty-five times by England, and a man who has played for Sunderland, Manchester City, Southampton, Derby and Notts County, together with a spell in Germany with Werder Bremen, was a centre half who was rarely dirty. He was a superb header of the ball, but was clean with his jump. So many players 'climb' or use their arms when going up for the ball. But not Watson.

Sunderland are a club – and a town – crying out for a successful soccer team. They have had one in the past and the passion for the game in the North East remains undiminished. They are waiting to explode. A crowd of only 15,000 at Roker Park creates a very special atmosphere. Leighton James, whose other clubs have included Burnley, Derby, QPR and Swansea, exhibited his skills on Wearside as he approached the twilight of his career. James is the type of player who always excites the crowds – always looking to run at opponents with the ball. His breed need protection, but James himself has a habit of kicking the ball past a defender and then charging straight into him, claiming obstruction and an indirect free kick.

I think it is true that every good side needs one iron man, but sometimes the reputation is far more fearsome than the actual article, and it does not have to be a defender. Referees must not be lulled into the theory that defenders are the real hit men of the game. Often it is the reverse. Forwards can create problems by illegal use of the arms or elbows, by pushing, shoving or kicking opponents and so on.

However, the more renowned iron men have usually been either defenders or midfield players. Jimmy Case, for example. He can be a fairly violent player. That can be seen from the number of cautions he has received over the years, and he must be watched carefully. Gerry Gow, whom I refereed in the FA Cup Final when he was with Manchester City and who caused me to be criticised in some quarters for not taking punitive action against him, was a mighty hard man. But that was his role – to put himself about and put the fear of God into opponents. Billy Bremner and Norman Hunter were recognised as the hard men of the Leeds United side under Don Revie but, towards the end of Revie's reign, Terry Yorath was probably worse than either of them. Tommy Smith, Ron Harris, Peter Storey, Jim Holton and, during my time of watching Sheffield Wednesday, Tony Kay. These men were all known to be hard. But I do not think they were cynical. Clumsy, maybe, but not cynical. They invariably had the ball in mind.

It is usual for players to show aggression towards members of the opposition, but, during the game between Manchester United and Brighton at Old Trafford in October 1979, I cautioned Brighton's goalkeeper Eric Steele and his team-mate Gary Williams. It was the first time in almost twenty years of refereeing that I had taken the names of two players on the same side for having a go at one another. It later transpired that blows had been exchanged. I did not, in fact, see any punches thrown – they would have been sent off, otherwise. As I told the Press at the time, 'I saw the number three grab hold of the goalkeeper. Something had obviously been said by the 'keeper and they were cautioned for showing an aggressive attitude towards each other. It officially qualifies as ungentlemanly conduct.' A referee cannot take action over something neither he nor his linesmen saw.

Another clash that surprised me was between Mike Channon and Peter Shilton at the start of a game between Norwich City and Southampton at Carrow Road in November 1983. Channon challenged Shilton late and unfairly and I gave a free kick to Southampton. Perhaps I went into the situation slightly unprepared, because Channon was playing against the club for whom he scored no fewer than 208 first-class goals and he and Shilton had been England team-mates on many occasions. I thought that they were bound to be friendly towards each other, but the atmosphere was decidedly unfriendly. The reaction of Shilton, who had taken a heavy knock, amazed me. He was fuming. I had to nurse that situation for the rest of the game. The ball had been loose and, in retrospect, it was clear that Channon achieved what he set out to do – and that was to 'clonk' Shilton. I vowed that I would never again automatically assume that players would be on good terms or prepared to forgive and forget simply because they had once played together.

When in conversation after matches, the subject often turns towards some of the great players from the past. Jimmy Greaves, Denis Law, Stanley Matthews and John Charles are some of the men I remember from my childhood and in more recent times. My personal idol as a youngster was Derek Dooley, and Don Megson, the Sheffield Wednesday full back, was another favourite. We regarded him as a tank, but a man who also possessed more than a modicum of skill.

All referees like to handle matches in which great players take part. I have officiated in matches involving Keegan, Robson, Dalglish and all the best players in English football in recent years. On my trips to the Continent as a FIFA referee, I have come across players such as Platini, Rummenigge and Boniek, and I have also refereed George Best – what a disappointment.

I was thrilled at the prospect of handling the game between Stoke City and Fulham at the Victoria Ground in November 1977. A seemingly routine Second Division match was hauled out of the ordinary by the fact that Best, quite possibly the most naturally-gifted footballer who has ever drawn breath, would be playing. Best, the nomadic talent, who transfixed crowds into breathless anticipation whenever he touched the ball. If ever a footballer can be a genius, George surely was. It was pouring with rain that day in the Potteries and Best, perhaps having lost that half-yard of acceleration that was fundamental to his brilliance at his peak, was uninspired and his workrate was appallingly low. I came off the field feeling slightly cheated.

I experienced similar emotions when I ran the line in a match in which Bobby Charlton was playing. It was Chester against Preston North End, the club he joined after his career at Manchester United was over. Bobby was a superb player, but my opinion of him was clouded slightly by his disputing every decision of importance given by Colin Seel, the referee, in the opening half an hour. Colin had been bubbling before the match because he was about to referee a match in which Bobby Charlton was playing. It was an ambition fulfilled, but when the game got under way, I was watching from the line and wondering who was running the match – Bobby Charlton or Colin Seel? After thirty minutes, Colin had to put his foot down. At half-time, Colin came into the dressing room a disappointed man. 'I really had to pull Charlton over the coals,' he said, 'and tell him to cut out his arguing. And I was so looking forward to this match.'

The Manchester City dressing room was full of fun during the seventies. Frannie Lee, Mike Summerbee, Rodney Marsh, Mike Channon and Colin Bell. All outstanding players who liked a laugh. They always seemed to be asking Channon which horse was going to win the next race at Newmarket.

Talking of Francis Lee, I recall going into the Arsenal dressing room at Derby's Baseball Ground to carry out a stud inspection. I was checking Frank McLintock's boots when he enquired whether I was aware that Lee, who was playing, was the 'best diver in the game'. It seemed to me that Frank, who had been a player for many years and indeed captained Arsenal to the League and FA Cup Double in season 1970-71, was attempting to pull the leg of this 'rookie' linesman. My response was, 'Oh yes, of course I know that. In fact, we've been instructed to take out not a flag, but a set of numbers to give Lee marks out of ten every time he goes down.' I think Frank got the message!

Also while I was a linesman, I remember covering a game between Newcastle and Wolves at St James's Park. Pat Howard, the Newcastle centre half, was having a good, old-fashioned battle with Derek Dougan.

Pushing, shoving and various other tricks were being employed by both players in an effort to win the ball. Watching this type of confrontation from the line was an essential part of my refereeing education. Eventually, Howard was cautioned, rather harshly in my opinion.

As a result, the officials had to attend a disciplinary hearing in Sheffield. Howard was supported by Joe Harvey, the Newcastle manager, and the chairman of the committee that day was Sir Matt Busby. Ernest Kangley, who had been such a major influence in my early refereeing days in Sheffield, was also on the panel. I must say that I left that meeting with a great sense of pride for, rightly in my view, the committee had decided that the caution was unjustified. Television evidence had substantiated this. Referee, linesmen, players and manager all received a fair hearing and the disciplinary panel made every effort to ensure the true facts were revealed. Afterwards, we retired to the bar and enjoyed a drink and a chat with no hard feelings. In fact we talked about the weather which, on the day of the match, had been appalling, with a swirling wind and pouring rain. Both Howard and Harvey had missed a day's training and incurred considerable expense, but they were most cordial.

9
The Managers

Football management is a precarious business and sometimes it shows. A manager leads a life akin to the man in the circus walking the tightrope. Not much of a wobble is required for him to fall. He has to please not only thousands of fickle supporters, but also his often even more demanding board of directors. He must exercise man-management skills, 'motivation' in the modern idiom, to bring out the best from his players. That type of pressure often manifests itself with visible displays of tension before and after a game.

Perhaps tension causes the frustration that leads to outbursts from managers who sometimes condemn referees as a bunch of amateurs operating in a professional environment. I believe many referees would give up their jobs to become full-time officials, paid appropriately and able to devote all their energies to improving their ability to handle football matches. But, as it is, referees spend a great deal of their free time training, discussing the laws of the game and travelling the length and breadth of the country attending seminars and refereeing associations to ensure that their experiences are shared.

A referee must recognise that at times, particularly when leaving the field of play, managers will dispute a decision. Avoid confrontation. Some managers, though, insist on pursuing their point. In February 1981, I refereed a game between Burnley and Exeter City. It started well but then, for some unaccountable reason, a number of Exeter players lost their heads and I was forced to caution seven of them. At the end of the game, the Exeter manager, Brian Godfrey, knocked on my dressing room door and asked to come in. I could sense that he was incensed, so I suggested he returned in twenty minutes or so by which time, I thought, he might have calmed down. Sure enough, he did come back, but he seemed to have lost none of his anger. As Godfrey was launching into his fusillade, I asked a local policeman into the dressing room to act as an independent witness. Godfrey disappeared, but not before he had said enough to become the only manager I have ever reported to the Football Association. He completely lost his head.

Eventually, the presence of the policeman and the realization that he might end up transgressing the laws of the land halted Godfrey on that occasion, and, indeed, managers often keep quiet if an official can bring to their attention the magnitude of their allegations. I did not come across Bobby Robson very frequently before he left Ipswich to become manager of England but, on one of those few occasions, Robson was left speechless following the interjection of one of my linesmen.

Middlesbrough were playing Ipswich at Ayresome Park and, towards the end of the game, I disallowed an Ipswich 'goal' for offside. At the conclusion of the match, Robson knocked on the door and I shouted, 'Come in.' He was absolutely seething. After we had been arguing about the decision for two or three minutes, Jim McAulay, the linesman whose raised flag had prompted me not to award the goal, stepped in and said, 'Mr Robson, are you calling me a cheat? I suggest you watch television tonight and look at the replay of the incident.' As far as Jim was concerned, that was the end of the conversation and Robson departed.

A referee can often predict the character of a manager he has never met before simply by seeing the team's attitude – particularly in the area of dissension. Managers who exercise strong discipline rarely put out a team whose players argue readily.

Fulham, under the management of Malcolm Macdonald, were a side who rarely disputed decisions, and that was a reflection of Malcolm's influence. I encountered him on a number of occasions during his days as a player. He had power and pace and the fans loved him. Macdonald was the man who arrived in a white Rolls Royce at St James's Park on the day he signed for Newcastle. Arrogant, maybe, but it was the type of stunt that endeared him to the soccer-mad Geordies on his first day in Tyneside. He became their hero on day one. But the game that stands out in my mind was when he had been transferred to Arsenal. They were playing Liverpool at Anfield and Steve Heighway was charging towards the Arsenal penalty area on one of his attacking runs. Macdonald, back to help his defence, deliberately tripped Heighway and the Liverpool player went crashing to the ground, rolled over three or four times and finished flat on his face. The incident was in front of the Kop and the crowd began chanting, 'Off! Off! Off!'

I said to Malcolm, 'Okay, you know what you've done. Just listen to them. They're baying for your blood.' And then a smile. I did not threaten him by saying that next time he would be cautioned or sent off. Malcolm, an intelligent individual, knew the score. When, a few years later, I handled a Fulham side under Malcolm's control, I was very impressed with the level of discipline in the team. It was clear Malcolm had instilled in his men the futility of constantly disputing the referee's decision. That approach, of course, makes life much easier for referees.

Strong management filters through to the players. Consequently, Nottingham Forest and Liverpool usually accept my decisions – largely because of the influence of Brian Clough and Bob Paisley and, more recently, Joe Fagan.

I have handled Forest on a number of occasions, yet had little contact with Clough, an indication of how rarely he interferes with referees and disputes their decisions. I do recall, however, being struck at the discipline Clough enforced in the dressing rooms of Forest and Derby County. When, during my time as a linesman on the Football League, I went in to check the players' studs, Clough instructed all his players to sit on the bench and stay there until I had completed my inspection. This was a great help and compared favourably with the chaos in some dressing rooms. Subsequently, when I have been refereeing Forest, my linesmen have more than once commented on the decorum Clough insists upon. When I began as a linesman in the Football League, it was compulsory to check all the players' studs before a match; now it is optional.

Other encounters with Clough that I recall include the 1979 League Cup semi-final when Forest beat Watford 3-1 on aggregate. I handled the goalless second leg, played on a Vicarage Road pitch which had been protected against frost by bundles of straw for a few days leading up to the match. Despite a slippery surface, the game was played in an excellent spirit, and Clough and his opposite number Graham Taylor were both delighted the match had been played and had some kind things to say about the way I handled the game.

Clough also delivered one of the finest speeches I have heard on the need for greater co-operation between referees and clubs. On that memorable Sunday morning at a meeting of the Association of Football League Referees and Linesmen at Warwick University, Clough, in his rousing oration, emphasised the need for referees to become more professional in their approach. His comments and observations were spot on and he certainly pulled no punches. His speech was well received and I can assure him that his visit to Warwick University was extremely worthwhile. When we have spoken, Clough has always talked a great deal of sense. He certainly cares about the game and its players.

Paisley, Fagan and Ronnie Moran and, formerly, Bill Shankly – a man of the people if ever there was one – have been a formidable management team. The club's system of allowing a lot of their players to learn the 'Liverpool way' in the Central League before thrusting them into the first team has been remarkably successful. Ian Rush, for instance, spent a couple of seasons in the reserves following his transfer from Chester. Shankly, Paisley, Fagan and Moran have never been afraid to pass comment to referees, but they do it quietly and politely, never over the top, and any referee would be a fool not to listen. They are not attempting to influence the referee's decision, just questioning why he has done something and giving him the opportunity to explain his reasons.

My first Merseyside 'derby' was in October 1980. The game was drawn 2-2 at Goodison Park and provided spectacular and skilful entertainment in a superb atmosphere. There was plenty of commitment from both sides, and the match took some handling at times, but the reactions from the players were all that an official could ask for. You can imagine my sense of pride when, the next day, I read that Paisley had said, 'I thought the referee was magnificent. I made a point of going to speak to him because in these games you can get carried away. But I thought he was superb. The record books will show a draw, but the winners have been the public and the game of football. The players, referee and spectators all contributed to a marvellous match.' The only shame was that, due to a strike, the television cameras scheduled to cover the match never appeared, so it was not recorded for posterity.

Gordon Lee, the Everton manager at the time of the match, was not so enthusiastic initially. He talked mainly about an isolated offside decision and said, 'The tempo was too fast and there was not enough quality football.' He later revised his verdict to, 'It was one hell of a match. The referee had to work hard because of the pace, but he deserves credit for keeping the game going.'

Lee, in my experience, developed something of a knack for criticising what everybody else thought was an outstanding game. One of the most exciting matches I have handled was a 4-4 draw between Everton and Newcastle United. The atmosphere was electric and the feast of football provided the type of entertainment fans love. To my amazement, though, Lee was extensively quoted in the newspapers the next day making unflattering remarks about the game. Lee, then manager of Everton and previously in charge at Newcastle, said there were too many defensive errors and that was not what football should be about. I could not believe it. Managers are often complaining about poor attendances and, when there was the type of game guaranteed to bring in the crowds, here was one of the managers knocking it down. Gordon Lee might not have enjoyed the game, but I am sure the thousands on the terraces did.

Tommy Docherty and Malcolm Allison are two of the most talked-about and controversial managers since the war. Outspoken, brash, egotistical and at times very, very right. As the saying goes, you either love them or hate them and nobody could accuse either of being uninteresting. I have had some close encounters with them both.

One of the finest matches I refereed in the early part of my Football League career was between Sunderland and Manchester United at Roker Park on Easter Monday, April 1977, during my second season as a Football League referee. Sunderland won a truly rousing encounter 2-1. Tommy Docherty, then the United manager, said afterwards in a radio interview with Desmond Lynam, who was working for BBC Radio at the time, 'The ref had a magnificent game.' I felt ten feet tall, even though Sunderland

manager Jimmy Adamson was not pleased that I had taken the names of two of his players, despite the fact that I also cautioned two from United in an effort to keep a stirring match in order. As I left the ground, pleased that Docherty thought I had helped contribute to a memorable match, a young boy asked for my autograph. I gladly signed on a piece of paper, which the youngster promptly tore to pieces right in front of my eyes, threw the scraps onto the floor and exclaimed, 'My dad thinks you're rubbish!'

Docherty has managed Chelsea, Rotherham, Aston Villa, Manchester United, Derby, Queen's Park Rangers three times, Preston and Wolves – quite apart from the Scottish national team and his overseas appointments, which have included FC Porto and Sydney Olympic. His first spell with QPR was in the late sixties. He then returned to Loftus Road in May 1979, was sacked and then reinstated before leaving for good in October 1980. During his latest stint at the club, I recall doing a League Cup match between Wolves and Rangers. Just twenty minutes of the match had elapsed when Docherty walked up the touchline, indicating that a substitution was about to take place and that Stan Bowles was the player he wanted to bring off. Stan, a highly skilful player but himself a bit of a tearaway, clearly saw this and started to run to the other side of the field, attempting to ignore his manager. I informed Bowles that The Doc wanted to replace him.

'I'm not going off,' he replied, 'I've only been on the park for twenty minutes.'

'But you're getting paid for this match. So surely it doesn't matter whether you play for twenty minutes or ninety,' I tried to reason. Stan just smiled at me and ran towards the touchline. I could see Bowles and Docherty walking back to the trainers' box arguing fiercely.

My meetings with Allison have not always been smooth. I remember one Monday morning picking up the *Daily Star* newspaper and reading an article by Allison, in which he claimed that millions of television viewers had seen Keith Hackett 'fall over himself' to avoid giving a penalty to Tottenham in an FA Cup match against Manchester United at White Hart Lane on the previous Saturday. I was quite pleased, really, because at least it showed I was not a 'homer'. Nevertheless, I thought it was wrong for somebody who had no connections with either club and, quite possibly, had not even been at the match to criticise my decisions – especially as both Spurs and United seemed pleased with what I had done in the game.

I had quite a 'set-to' with Allison early in 1983. It all started when I received a call at about half past nine one Saturday morning. It was Middlesbrough FC and they were ringing to tell me that they thought the pitch was unplayable for the match against Crystal Palace that afternoon. This amazed me because, on the Friday, they said the pitch was perfectly acceptable and there was no need for me to travel overnight. What was more, the overnight forecast had not predicted rain. Clearly, whoever had looked at the pitch on the Friday had made an error of judgement. Anyway, I jumped in my car and drove to Ayresome Park.

When I walked out at about ten thirty on the Saturday morning to look at the pitch, I did not have to think hard to reach my decision. Water covered the playing surface to a depth of two inches in places. The groundsman was convinced that there was no chance of the match being played and I agreed with him. It was an absolute quagmire. I liaised with the Middlesbrough secretary and the Football League and, between us, we decided that the game could not go ahead. I asked where the Palace team was. Unfortunately, they were on the train, but the Middlesbrough secretary said, 'Leave it to me. I'll try to get hold of them.'

With my job completed, I decided to leave. I was walking out of the ground towards my car, with a bag in one hand and my shirt on a hanger in the other, when I was met by Allison getting out of a Jaguar.

'What's the problem?' he asked with some suprise.

'The game's off,' I replied. But he just could not accept that. He wanted to start an argument there and then in the middle of the road.

I said, 'Look, I don't care what you think. I'm the guy who's actually been out on the field. Look at my Wellingtons – they're covered in mud. You haven't even looked at the pitch. I've made the decision along with the Football League to call this match off. And that is the end of the story. I'm going home.'

On another occasion I was refereeing the FA Cup third round match in January 1981 in which Allison made his first trip back to Manchester City since being sacked three months earlier. He was by now in charge of Crystal Palace. There was a tremendous buzz around the stadium and Allison received a rapturous reception from the home supporters as he walked out onto the Maine Road pitch with both arms raised aloft. The end result, though, was not so welcoming for Big Mal – Manchester City 4, Crystal Palace 0.

Lawrie McMenemy, Ron Atkinson and Ron Saunders are three of the most successful managers of recent years. McMenemy, the affable Geordie who put the former soccer backwater of Southampton on the map before moving to his native Sunderland, is an ex-guardsman who never played soccer in the Football League, which makes his achievements all the more remarkable. Players often do not respond to managers who have not 'done it' themselves. Big Lawrie, who became the longest-serving manager in the League, has done it in management alright. Under his guidance, Southampton finished in the highest League position in their history and, when a Second Division club, beat mighty Manchester United in the final to win the FA Cup in 1976, thanks to a goal by Bobby Stokes.

I first met Lawrie when he was manager of Grimsby. His team were playing Bury and I was running the line, from where an official usually sees more of the managers than the man in the middle. Bobby Smith, the Bury manager, was sitting in the dug-out hurling a whole stream of comments. His particular target was referee John Yates who, at the time, had developed quite a reputation for cautioning players. Personally, I always found Yates fair, if very firm. Smith's remarks became progressively more vociferous and his actions more animated. Eventually, he climbed out of the trainers' box and moved towards the touchline. I asked him on a couple of occasions to return to his seat, but he refused to move and I was about to take action by calling over the referee, when McMenemy resolved the problem. He had been sitting in his own dug-out, watching Smith and he said, 'I think you'd better sit down and keep quiet or otherwise you're going to find yourself in trouble.'

McMenemy is usually considered one of soccer's nice guys and he comes across well when being interviewed. But when one looks at recent Southampton teams, they are a hard lot. There is no doubt that they have been one of the more difficult teams in the Football League to control, with players such as Steve Williams and Mick Mills, both of whom were never averse to disputing my decisions.

Atkinson has both the easiest and most difficult managerial job in football. Easy because he already has a glittering array of international talent at his disposal and the Old Trafford coffers are rarely short of more money to strengthen his squad; difficult because Atkinson must satisfy the largest club following in football. They demand success. They will not be satisfied until United become the premier team in England and it is Atkinson's burning desire to achieve just that. The 1983 FA Cup final triumph over Brighton after a replay partially erased Atkinson's disappointment at losing that year's Milk Cup Final to Liverpool. And they triumphed again over Everton in 1985. But what the United fans – like those from all the major clubs – consider the ultimate achievement is the League Championship.

Ron has a tremendous responsibility. Wherever I travel in the world to referee, people are asking me about Manchester United. How good is their current team? Does it compare with the Busby Babes? Or with the era of

Best, Charlton and Law? The first time I met Atkinson was during his Cambridge days. I am sure a man like Atkinson, who has been manager of a club in the lower divisions, has a full appreciation of money and club finances, even though he now has millions at his disposal at Old Trafford. Ron is a good communicator and certainly seems to be able to get his team bubbling.

There was an occasion in May 1983 when, during United's 3-0 defeat against Arsenal at Highbury, referee Eric Read banished Atkinson from the touchline for excessive comments. I have never had problems with Ron shouting from the dug-out, and there are ways and means of handling that type of situation. There are bound to be times during a game, no matter who the referee is, when a decision or an injury to a player infuriates a manager. It is important that the referee does not overreact. Quite often the polite approach, playing down the whole thing, is the most effective way of placating an irate manager; sometimes a more dictatorial attitude is necessary, especially if the initial 'soft' manner fails. It is up to the referee to make the judgement. I would like to think that, if I was confronted by Atkinson or any other manager who wanted to come to the touchline and dispute or argue, I could handle the situation without having to 'send off' the manager.

Atkinson has a flash exterior in many people's view. They think he dresses too extravagantly. But, to me, he always looks smart and, anyway,

the clothes he chooses to wear are his business. The important thing is that
he always acts in a relaxed and civil manner when he brings in the
teamsheets before the kick-off. He seems to be enjoying himself, although
inside his stomach might be turning over with nerves.

Ron Saunders is the man who, in 1980-81, took Aston Villa to their first
League Championship success for seventy-one years. Ron developed a
reputation as a hard man during the early part of his management career
by punishing the players through tortuous training routines at Norwich.
He has done little to erase that determined, unsmiling image. If ever there
was a realist, it is surely this man. So it came as something of a surprise
when I arrived at Birmingham, where he became manager after leaving
Villa, to discover that he had ordered a cross to be painted on the
floodlights in an attempt to rid St Andrew's of a curse that was apparently
haunting the place. Even the players had crosses painted on the side of
their boots, much to their amusement as they ran on to the pitch. I
understand Saunders also brought in a gypsy to rid the ground of its curse.

After another game at St Andrew's, in which Birmingham played Spurs,
Saunders knocked on our dressing room door after the game and
presented the three officials with a Birmingham City tie. 'You'll probably
never want to wear them,' he joked, 'but thanks anyway.' This was after a

goalless draw, but by no means a dull one. Both teams had received a standing ovation at the end of a fiercely competitive match. Saunders' action was the complete antithesis of his reputation. He puts on a hard, unsmiling image, but deep down I think he is a good-hearted fellow.

An excellent means of improving one's refereeing at the highest level is by talking to Football League managers, and there are a number who stand out in mind as men always prepared to pass on constructive advice and criticism. They appreciate the need for a close relationship between players, managers and arbiters.

Jack Charlton is often outspoken in his view that referees lack professionalism. I recall, when Big Jack was manager of Middlesbrough, having a line appointment at Ayresome Park in the fifth round of the FA Cup. Gordon Hill, that excellent referee and a man who had a tremendous rapport with players and managers, was in the middle. After the game Jack, who more than once stated that he thought Gordon was the 'players' ref', knocked at the dressing room door and invited us upstairs for a drink. We had a highly informative and convivial conversation on that occasion and I learned a great deal from it. But I do not think that the way Jack often gave the impression that he thought referees were a bunch of amateurs – often right to officials' faces – was conducive to good relations between managers and referees.

Harry Haslam was a manager always prepared to talk at length. While he was manager of Sheffield United, Harry invited me in on a couple of occasions to talk to the team in an effort to reduce the amount of dissension they were showing on the field. United players were receiving a large number of cautions and I was instructed to outline the referee's side of the story and ways in which players could avoid dissent. A smile was rarely far from Harry's face and he was chiefly responsible for the influx of South American players to the Football League at the latter end of the seventies. Indeed, the story goes that, if he could have raised just a few thousand pounds more, he would have signed Diego Maradona.

Mick Buxton, who has performed wonders as manager of Huddersfield, is another who has impressed me as a marvellous communicator. He attended a meeting of the Association of Football League Referees and Linesmen, Yorkshire section, and his telling talk provided an insight into the problems faced by players and managers in relation to refereeing decisions. He wants cheats out of the game as much as referees do.

Colin Murphy, now with Stockport County, is another who falls into this category. There have been times when I have handled a game and one of my decisions has gone against Colin, yet this has not clouded our discussions. He is prepared to talk openly about a referee's performance. I would always welcome a couple of hours in his company, because I am sure my refereeing would benefit.

One of my early recollections of discussion with a League manager was in my supplementary season. The League were running a system whereby a referee had to handle eight matches as a supplementary and, if he achieved reasonable marks and satisfied the League, he was invited to become a fully-fledged Football League referee. After a couple of games in my supplementary season, I went down with an Achilles tendon injury and was out of action for eight weeks. My return game was in early January between Lincoln City and Peterborough United. Quite a local 'derby' and, to my amazement, the cameras of Yorkshire Television were at the match. Although I had been training hard, I was still concerned whether my injury would hold out. Another relapse, I thought, might jeopardise my chances of getting onto the full League list.

The match went very well for me, and at the end, Lincoln manager Graham Taylor, who was later to lead Watford from Fourth Division to First in five seasons, came into my dressing room with some words of praise. That gave my confidence a great lift at that early stage of my League career.

A lot of people have criticised Watford's style of play under Taylor, in which they largely by-pass the midfield and attempt to get the ball into their opponents' penalty area as quickly and frequently as possible. To me, though, it is very exciting and not necessarily a retrograde step because it does not encourage individual skill. As far as Watford and Taylor are concerned, the most important thing is that it works. And it certainly does. In their first season in Division One, in 1982-83, Watford finished second in the League and the following season appeared in the FA Cup Final.

Taylor very much comes into the category of young, progressive-thinking managers who are excellent communicators. David Pleat, Luton's energetic manager, is another and, when one looks around the Football League, the trend is growing. Terry Venables, who has done so well at Barcelona, Alan Mullery and Macdonald were in the same mould and all were keen to forge stronger links between managers and referees. They both offered and listened to advice, aware that we could learn from each other. All have been successful at some stage of their career.

Taylor, as mentioned, guided Watford through the League from Fourth Division to First, and then led his side out at Wembley. Pleat was in charge at Luton when they gained promotion to the First Division in 1982 and his attractive sides have included some of the most exciting young players in the game, like Paul Walsh, Brian Stein and Ricky Hill, each of whom has played for the full England side.

Venables, who has been coach of the England under-21 team and a possible future England manager, is a man of many talents. He led Rangers to the FA Cup Final, the Second Division Championship and Europe in successive seasons before his move to Spain.

When Brighton gained promotion to Division One for the first time in their history in 1979, Mullery was the manager at the Goldstone Ground. Macdonald steered Fulham to promotion from the Third Division and, the following season, they finished just a point adrift of third-placed Leicester at the top of the Second Division.

Ian Greaves, whose managerial appointments have included Huddersfield, Bolton, Oxford and Wolves is an excellent communicator, too. He is always prepared to spend time chatting to the referee, even if the result has gone against his team, as it did on a number of occasions when I refereed games involving Greaves' side. He might only be passing the time of day, but it all helps to build up amenable relations between managers and officials. Greaves would always thank the officials with a nod of appreciation.

Peter Taylor, for so long Brian Clough's partner at Derby and Nottingham Forest, and later on his own at the Baseball Ground, is willing, to talk at length after a game. In the Forest days, it was usually Taylor who said more to the referee than Clough, who was probably involved in the dressing room with his players.

Other managers go out of their way to prevent their players becoming involved in a potentially explosive situation. I remember Jim Smith, who did such a magnificent job as boss of Oxford, doing just that during my days on the Northern Premier League. Indeed, it was my first refereeing appointment on the NPL and Boston United were playing Matlock. During the course of the game, Billy Howells, a hard-tackling half back with Boston, was creating a few problems with his strong challenges and noisy outbursts. I was poised to answer back following another verbal confrontation, when Jim ran towards Billy and shouted that he should keep his mouth shut and get on with the game. 'Don't you realise this lad is from Sheffield?' bellowed Jim, who, like me, was Sheffield-born. I refereed Boston on a number of occasions and subsequently teams under Jim's control in the League. Jim, a hard man, is always honest and constructive in his criticism of referees.

I remember refereeing Birmingham once, shortly after Smith had taken them over, in a match at Newcastle. Birmingham had lost the game, when they should not have done so. They had thrown it away. The officials were some distance away from the Birmingham dressing room, but we could hear Jim shouting at his players. He was giving them a terrible grilling. But his methods seem to work because Jim can usually get the best out of his players.

Alan Oakes enjoyed an enormously long career in the Football League – a record 565 appearances for Manchester City, a further 211 for Chester and then one for Port Vale, his latter appearances being mostly as player-manager. Being on the field and attempting to remain objective, like any manager must, is surely one of the most difficult tasks, yet Oakes was a successful player-manager. From the referee's point of view, his most endearing trait was his ability to calm players down. One of his own team might be close to bursting point, yet a quiet word from Alan would almost invariably have the desired calming effect. All the time, of course, he would be concentrating hard on his own game, attempting not to make a mistake with the ball.

If I had been a good player and then chosen to go into management, I do not think I would have combined the two simultaneously. John Toshack had a highly successful time as player-manager, leading Swansea from Divisions Four to One in four seasons – one quicker even than Watford under Taylor. But things did not work out quite so well for Alan Ball in his attempts at the dual role. I remember refereeing Carlisle against Blackpool. Ball was Blackpool's player-manager at the time and we clashed. During the course of the game, one of Ball's players struck a member of the opposition. It was a clear punch but, when I took action, Ball lost his temper. For the rest of the game, he kept telling me that I had made a mistake and how upset he was. Ball was the type of player who became naturally involved in a match and I think he found it difficult to remain objective. Subsequently, Ball has done well at Portsmouth when concentrating exclusively on being a manager and not playing.

There have certainly been other managers with whom I have clashed. Ken Knighton, for example. Knighton, who has managed Sunderland, Orient and non-League Dagenham, agreed with my decision to dismiss his defender Joe Bolton for striking Terry Cochrane during Sunderland's 1-0 defeat against neighbours Middlesbrough at Ayresome Park in February 1981, but he had something to say about my awarding a free kick to 'Boro, from which they scored their decisive goal. Knighton's response to the eagerly-awaiting newspaper reporters was, 'The one clear-cut chance of the game was created by the referee, when he gave the free kick the wrong way. I would like to invite him into my house, give him a glass of beer, set him down in front of the television to watch the incident, and then see if he still thinks it was a free kick to Middlesbrough.' Personally, I would have liked to have had that beer and convivial chat with Knighton after the game.

Knighton could lose his composure. Like a number of managers, Knighton is the sort who likes to stand at the tunnel entrance and make comments in the hope that the referee will not take action, or perhaps throw a few accusing glances. Managers are always reluctant actually to enter the inner sanctum of the officials' dressing room because they are aware that they would then be risking a lot.

Jimmy Adamson, who also spent a segment of his managerial career at Roker Park, is another who has left more than one referee with a flea in his ear. I have already mentioned his discontent when I cautioned two of his players during that marvellous game against Manchester United in 1977. Before that, Adamson was at Burnley and on one occasion I was running the line for Ken Burns, an international referee and a man whom I respected enormously. As we were walking up the tunnel at Turf Moor, Adamson called Burns a 'cheat'. Burns kept quiet, doing his best to ignore Adamson. Adamson repeated his accusation and the word 'cheat' was uttered on two or three further occasions, but Ken was prepared to let it pass, dismissing it as something that happened in the heat of the moment. But then the other linesman said something and the whole incident suddenly exploded. The result was that Adamson was reported to the Football Association. I found Adamson a difficult man, the sort of chap who always looked as though he wanted to say something.

Alan Durban, yet another former Sunderland manager, can be very outspoken. The Wearside public are extremely demanding, and Durban's task was not an easy one. In his time at Roker Park, the club were usually attempting to avoid relegation rather than challenging at the top of the table. There is no doubt, though, that Durban can be to the point when speaking to referees.

I clashed with one-time Wrexham manager Arfon Griffiths after I had awarded that penalty, mentioned elsewhere, against his team when Joey Jones tugged Newcastle player John Brownlie's shirt. Griffiths was critical of my decision. He did not actually come into the dressing room, but he was annoyed and making various noises as we were going up the tunnel. Like many managers, he was not actually addressing his remarks directly to me, but speaking to somebody else as a 'decoy' to vent his feelings.

I remember refereeing Everton v Watford in January 1983. Adrian Heath of Everton was brought down by Joe Bolton in the opening minutes of the match. At that time, players were being sent off for 'professional fouls' but I decided a cautioning for ungentlemanly conduct would suffice, especially considering that a strong swirling wind had contributed to Bolton's foul. I did not think the offence warranted a dismissal, but that was not the way Howard Kendall, the Everton manager, saw it. He stated that I had been weak and should have sent Bolton off. His argument to the Press was that, earlier in the season, one of his players, Glenn Keeley, had been dismissed for a similar offence in the local 'derby' against Liverpool, which Everton lost 5-0. I was not being consistent with referee Derek Civil's decision in that match, claimed Kendall.

Bob Stokoe, who has managed Rochdale, Blackpool and Carlisle each twice, as well as Charlton, Sunderland and Bury, can lose his rag. The highlight of his career was when he led Sunderland, then in the Second Division, to victory over Leeds United in the 1973 FA Cup Final. I remember him walking onto the pitch, arms aloft Bill Shankly style, after the semi-final victory over Arsenal at Hillsborough, when I was a spectator. Stokoe becomes totally wrapped up in a game and can show a great disdain towards referees. He can get uptight both during and after a match and finds it difficult to restrain himself.

The man who scored Sunderland's winning goal against Leeds at Wembley was Ian Porterfield, who himself has entered the precarious field of management. I am sure Ian will have to live with that goal for the rest of his life, but there could be plenty worse things to be remembered for. I have been involved more with Sheffield United than any other club, giving talks and so on. Consequently, I have seen at first hand the type of pressure Ian is under. He is at a big club that should not be in the lower divisions. His target, therefore, must always be promotion, and nobody can deny that Ian has not placed United firmly on the road to recovery. Ian is a fairly deep-thinking man and, by seeing him in his day-to-day working environment and the type of responsibility he has on his shoulders, one can appreciate why managers sometimes become frustrated. This must be borne in mind when dealing with them on match day.

A referee can go out looking for controversy, but that is wrong. I am not necessarily saying that refs should slip in to the ground, handle the match, and slip out equally quietly, without murmuring a word, but our duty is to allow the paying public to get value for money watching the star players. The bloke in black should not be the star turn. We are not encouraged to swap dialogue with managers. The time to do that is when at seminars, dinners, award presentations and the like, functions that perhaps benefit a club's finances or support a charity.

While some managers simply reel off a string of fairly meaningless platitudes and clichés merely to appease a questioner when sitting on these panels, Billy Bremner enters the discussion in the right spirit. I was sitting on a panel with him at Rotherham United and he was superb. A schoolboy asked Billy a question and, instead of ignoring or deflecting the issue, he answered it in great depth. Billy had some cogent thoughts on the game at boys' level. His concern was that everybody wants to win a trophy and there are so many cups and prizes to be won by boys that, at the end of even a moderate season, a youngsters' team's trophy cabinet could be bulging with silverware. Rewards were available when a side had not really earned them. Billy thought there was a danger that it could instil a 'this-is-easy' attitude in prospective professionals at an early age.

This perceptive, caring and articulate means of getting over his views contrasted with Bremner's tigerish attitude on the pitch. One could always see that he never took anything for granted. I bet he never thought, 'This is easy.' Billy, who seems to be building a successful management career, always played to win. I first encountered him while he was playing for Hull. Billy's enthusiasm was going beyond acceptable bounds and I was forced to stop the game and say to him, 'I am the referee and you are out here to play. Leave me to get on with my job and I'll allow you to get on with yours.' At that, there seemed to be a mutual 'disarmament' agreement and he presented few subsequent problems in the match.

On another occasion, I took a testimonial game at Bramall Lane. During the second half, Billy's team claimed an offside. As the linesman had not flagged, I ordered play to go on and anyway, everyone had agreed before the start that I should keep the game flowing as much as possible. But Bremner ran towards me and spouted a huge outburst of dissent. For the remainder of the match he would not leave that decision alone. The match was designed to raise money and entertain the crowd. Nothing was at stake, yet Billy was giving it everything, his attitude was professional and unyielding. That summed him up. Whenever he was on a pitch wearing football kit, Billy badly wanted to win.

Allan Clarke is another ex-Leeds player from the Don Revie era who impressed me in his attitude to young footballers. In the past few years, I have visited various clubs and lectured the apprentices on some aspects of the laws of the game. At the end of the session, the youngsters take a written examination to discover how conversant they are with the laws and their interpretation. I have been to Elland Road more than once and

Clarke, when he was manager there, always ensured that the entire operation was conducted in a highly professional manner. We were given the use of a good room in which the lecture could take place and all the necessary equipment was set up. Clarke insisted that all the young players were given a hot, nourishing meal at lunchtime. Some of those youngsters are now in the first team. Clarke has always given the impression of being a dour individual, but he is deep-thinking and clearly all the professionalism he learned under Revie rubbed off.

Jimmy Sirrel, the Scotsman who has spent so much of his managerial career at Notts County, is another who presents a dour front. Sirrel is the subject of a story that has passed around among referees. I could not vouch with certainty as to its veracity. Somehow, I have my doubts. Anyway, whenever Jimmy comes into the dressing room with the teamsheets, he always wants to examine the ball. He presses it and bounces it two or three times. It is habit, really, nothing else. But the story goes that one day the opposition manager persuaded the referee to take in a medicine ball with him. So, when Sirrel asked for the match ball, he was handed this weighty spheroid. When he attempted to bounce it, the ball plunged to the floor with a resounding thud. 'I don't know what things are coming to,' said the other manager. 'We're bound to get two or three players with broken ankles if we have to play with that thing!'

The media have created an image of flamboyance around John Bond, and I am sure he has done nothing to allay his reputation for jokes and jewellery, champagne and cigars. The trouble is that people look at him and say, 'He's a big mouth.' I have refereed teams with which Bond has been involved and, to me, he remains a genuine individual. At the end of the second of the two Centenary FA Cup Final matches, I was standing by the touchline when John got off his seat and thanked me for my performance in the two games. For me, that was one of the highlights of the occasion. The losing manager, bitterly disappointed, going out of his way to thank me. On another occasion, I recall handling a friendly match on a Monday night at Bramall Lane, which was agreed as part of the deal that took John Ryan from Sheffield United to Manchester City. It was just before Bond quit City and the previous Saturday, I had taken City in a League match against Coventry. To my surprise, John popped his head round the dressing room door just to wish me all the best for the game and say, 'I thought you had a good game on Saturday. We enjoyed it and I hope we'll enjoy it again tonight. I'll tell the lads to play it sensibly.'

Bond's approach contrasts with that of his successor at Norwich, Ken Brown. I have never had any problems with Ken, whose quiet manner is none the poorer for lacking Bond's bravado. Brown never criticises my performance or disputes a decision. He just gets on with his job and says that his responsibility is to run a football club and not to try to administer the laws.

Gordon Milne, that modest and unassuming individual, is also a man who rarely grabs headline space in newspapers, yet he is a hugely respected figure in the game. He was an excellent player and I remember him in his pre-Football League days with Wigan. Subsequently, when in charge of Coventry and Leicester, Gordon has got on with his job in a quiet and efficient manner. I have always found him extremely helpful when I have needed teamsheets and he retains an admirable degree of silence about the referee's performance, no matter how much he might be fuming internally.

After a couple of months of the 1983-84 season, few people would have given Leicester a chance of avoiding relegation, but they climbed to almost halfway. Milne did a superb job as manager. His team's level of fitness and workrate was high and they had the desire to escape the dreaded drop. Yet effort and commitment were not Leicester's sole allies – Milne's team possessed no mean skill.

Nevertheless, I sometimes wonder whether the English game is played at too fast a pace. A lot of emphasis is placed on running and stamina, with the skill factor often being neglected. Take the national team, for example. When England play Scotland, Northern Ireland and Wales – although these clashes are going to be less frequent following the abolition of the British Championship – the games are full of passion and pace. There is a lot of pride at stake and nobody wants to lose. England's matches in the European Championships and World Cup qualifying stages are of huge importance and, again, this tends to stunt the deployment of skill. Even England's friendly matches are usually against top-quality opposition.

I have often thought that, perhaps, England should play weaker opposition and more regular games, giving us a better chance of winning with an increase in confidence the result. It should be the same as in boxing. A good young heavyweight prospect does not go in with Muhammad Ali after just a couple of bouts, and England should not have to keep facing Brazil, Argentina and West Germany. The team should get three or four wins under their belts before playing the top sides.

For me, there can never be too much football. I love it. But I sometimes wonder whether coaches and managers can maintain sufficient variety in their training methods to overcome a certain staleness among players. They train every day, play matches often twice a week and, to them, it is a job. Tedium can certainly set in, no matter how glamorous it sounds, but I am sure that no job – be it pop star, Prime Minister, factory worker or footballer – is without its tiresome moments.

Referees appreciate congratulation. Not necessarily in an egotistic way, but because it shows that managers have noticed the way we are performing. I believe any contact between officials and clubs can do nothing but augment our ability. Sure, it is pleasing to my pride to be told how well I have done by a manager who has made a special point of approaching me, but more important is the forging of stronger bonds.

I received a certain amount of praise from John Neal – the Geordie who earned success in charge of Chelsea – during his time at Middlesbrough. A couple of weeks after handling an exciting match between 'Boro and Manchester United, a business colleague sent me a cutting from the local Middlesbrough newspaper in which Neal paid me the kind compliment of saying, 'Hackett was a referee who really took control. He was the boss. You just didn't notice him. In fact, you didn't think about him until he was mentioned after the game, and that's the acid test.' Neal always gives me a nod of acknowledgement when we meet or he brings in the teamsheets.

Referees must be conscious of the fact that coaches, probably rather than managers, attempt to manipulate the laws to their advantage. It is part of their job, but we must make certain they do not bend the law to the point where it is broken. For example, coaches will often encourage their players to complain that the 'wall' at a free kick has not retreated ten yards and, while the referee is sorting it out, the ball suddenly flies into the back of the net. The attacking team is claiming a goal, but the referee must be strong enough to say, 'No goal. I hadn't blown the whistle.'

I suppose these are acceptable tactics. Just a little bit of gamesmanship. But bribery would not be acceptable. I have never been offered money or any other form of incentive to award my decisions in favour of one team. If a manager ever came into the dressing room with a thousand pounds and asked me to 'help' his team, I would tell him to 'get lost' and report him immediately to the FA. I can state categorically that no form of bribery exists in the Football League these days. It would be a fraud on the public. I used to watch Sheffield Wednesday from the Kop at Hillsborough during the fifties and sixties and, like so many others, was shocked and disappointed when Peter Swan, Tony Kay – both England internationals – and 'Bronco' Layne, Wednesday's bustling centre forward, were all banned for life following the 'fixing' scandal. Men who had been heroes of mine had their careers stopped overnight. Wednesday went through enormous upheavals at the time and the game, quite rightly, was quick to react. People pay money to come and watch football and spend hours talking about it. The game would lose enormous credibility if bribing was discovered to be going on.

Coming from Sheffield, the League would never ask me to handle matches involving either Wednesday or United and it is rare indeed for me to do a match in which a club from Yorkshire is participating. Nevertheless, the League operate a zonal system among referees in an effort to minimise travelling time and expense. Consequently, most of my games are in the North of England and Midlands. However, I work in Romford, which is at the London end of Essex, usually travelling home to Sheffield at weekends, so most of my midweek appointments are in and around the capital.

Under Terry Neill's managership, Arsenal were undoubtedly the most successful team in London in the second half of the seventies. They reached three consecutive FA Cup Finals in 1978, 1979 and 1980 – the first team in the twentieth century to achieve the feat. I remember Neill walking into the dressing room with Bob Paisley to hand in the teamsheets before the 1980 semi-final at Hillsborough. I am relatively short in what I have to say to managers before a game. I just want to check the teams, confirm the goalkeepers and make certain there are no shirt colour clashes. But just as the pair were leaving, I wished them luck and hoped they would enjoy the game. 'Enjoy the game?' said Neill, who was always immaculately dressed, 'We'll be dying out there. It's a bloody semi-final. How can we enjoy it?'

I have nothing hard to say against Neill. Don Howe, for so long Neill's lieutenant at Highbury and the man who took over as manager when Neill was dismissed late in 1983, did most of the shouting from the touchline. Howe is another who thinks deeply about the game and its tactics and has the potential to pass on considerable worthwhile advice to both referees and other management staff.

Tottenham took over the mantle as London's top team from Arsenal in the early eighties. Spurs won the FA Cup themselves in 1981 and 1982. After the first of those Finals, when they beat Manchester City following a replay, their then manager Keith Burkinshaw was generous in his thanks to me. Burkinshaw is a Yorkshireman, talks straight but, in my experience, was not unduly blunt.

West Ham have also been successful in the Cup in recent years, winning at Wembley in both 1975 and 1980. John Lyall, their manager on both those occasions, is very much a gentleman and has helped to extend the club's reputation as a 'family club' who play attacking and attractive football.

Lyall's predecessor was Ron Greenwood, who left Upton Park in 1977 to become manager of England. I ran the line in West Ham matches during Greenwood's time there and it was evident that he had few problem players on his staff. Flair was an essential criterion when selecting his team or making additions to the West Ham squad.

Another mighty managerial figure from the past is Sir Matt Busby. He and Jimmy Murphy formed perhaps the first management partnership and their success was just reaching its peak when the Busby Babes were struck down in 1958. Busby is well-respected wherever you go in the game. I have come across him at disciplinary hearings. When Matt sat on the commission, deciding the fate of a player, he has always struck me as level-headed, a perceptive interrogator and keen to discover the truth. He has no pre-conceived ideas when he first walks into the room.

Disciplinary hearings, in fact, have been known to cause confrontation between managers and referees. A few years ago, I attended one such meeting at the Football Association's headquarters at Lancaster Gate, London. I had been the linesman in a match between Hull City and Manchester United, during which Alf Wood, the Hull centre forward, had been booked by referee Ray Tinkler. The disciplinary committee ruled that Wood, having exceeded his permitted quota of cautions, should be suspended. As we were about to catch the tube at Lancaster Gate underground station, the Hull manager John Kaye challenged us. He completely lost his temper, claiming we – and Tinkler in particular – were responsible for his player's ban. Ray managed to calm him down in expert fashion and the way he dealt with the problem gave me an eye-opener into how to pacify a truculent manager.

Another successful management team in Manchester was Joe Mercer and Malcolm Allison at Maine Road. Since Allison 'went it alone' in management, I have certainly had a few contretemps with him, but his mentor, Mercer, had a highly relaxed demeanour when I met him during my days as a linesman.

Jimmy Armfield, an outstanding player with Blackpool and England and later manager of Leeds, is a boss from the past who has impressed me with his manner. I ran the line during his time at Elland Road and he was never anything other than polite and pleasant. I never heard him criticise a referee and he was very much one of the old school in his approach. His problem might have been that he was not sufficiently ruthless to be successful in management. I enjoy listening to Armfield's comments on the radio. As an ex-player and manager, he has clearly acquired a deep knowledge of the game and this comes through.

Sometimes, it was difficult to believe that Frank O'Farrell was manager of Manchester United. He was quiet, almost reserved in his manner, and yet he was in charge of possibly the most famous football club in the world. Dave Sexton was much along the same lines. These two contrast with the more outgoing personalities of other United managers Tommy Docherty and Ron Atkinson.

The Referees

Players and managers are not the only people involved with soccer who gain reputations – notorious or otherwise. By the very nature of the game, referees, the men who make the decisions on the pitch, are bound to arouse strong emotions. No player, manager or fan of a club is likely to think too favourably of a referee who awards a dubious or critical decision in favour of the opposition. Nevertheless, some referees manage to avoid great controversy throughout their entire careers, while others almost appear to go out of their way to invite controversy and debate. None more so than Clive Thomas.

I have run the line for Clive and been very impressed with the accuracy of his decisions, but I have been less impressed with his attitude towards his linesmen. The very essence of referee-linesman co-operation is that the three officials work as a team, but Thomas has an air of authority towards his linesmen that borders on arrogance. It can be off-putting to the men with the flags.

Clive's knowledge and application of the laws and their interpretation is irreproachable. There is no doubt about that, but his man management is not always faultless. Indeed, especially in the early part of his career, he managed players almost by confrontation. Many people believe Clive made a conscious effort to court controversy, receive attention and get his name in print or on the air, but it must be remembered that Clive handles an exceptionally high proportion of top matches – frequently on television – and any controversial decisions he makes in those matches are bound to be brought to the public eye more than similar decisions made by another referee in a largely anonymous Fourth Division match.

He also tends to go out on a limb. Nothing illustrated this more than when, during the West Ham v Manchester United 'live' television match at Upton Park in November 1983, he was literally dragging players away from their celebrations in front of the fans on the terraces. Referees are always told never to handle players, but I am sure Clive thought seriously about the possible consequences of excessive celebrations after a goal – crowd trouble and time-wasting, for example. But, instead of liaising with the rest of the Association of Football League Referees and Linesmen and saying what he intended doing, he just went out and did it in front of the biggest audience he could find. It reeked of a stunt for the benefit of the 'live' television cameras.

He certainly brings referees more attention, and there is no doubt that some of the things he has said have been proved correct. I remember him saying many years ago that there were too many cheats in the game. This provoked quite a furore at the time, but I now understand what he was saying. The player who attempts to con the referee is a cheat. There was an occasion, of course, when Thomas accused West Ham manager John Lyall of calling him a cheat. The incident occurred at the end of the 1981 League Cup Final, shortly after Thomas had allowed Alan Kennedy's goal for Liverpool – despite the fact that Sammy Lee was lying prostrate in the penalty area in an offside position and almost directly in line with Kennedy's shot. Thomas ruled that Lee was not interfering with play.

I think most people were astonished when Lyall was alleged to have uttered the word 'cheat' to Thomas. It is one of the most offensive things that anybody can say to a referee, worse than the most abusive language. Lyall, in my experience, is a gentleman. He is honest and most people in the game hold him in the highest esteem. He is not the sort of manager who normally passes comment to referees. But, maybe on this one heated occasion, he lost his rag. If he did, I still blame Clive Thomas. He should not have been anywhere near the West Ham manager. He must have appreciated that Lyall would be on edge and to be close to him was tantamount to inciting trouble. Referees and linesmen should always keep well away from managers at the end of matches.

However, nobody can dispute the success Thomas has had in the game. Before retiring at the end of the 1983-84 season, he was at the top for more than a decade and refereed in the 1978 World Cup Finals in Argentina. Even then, he was involved in one of the most controversial incidents of the tournament. Brazil were playing Sweden and, in the dying seconds, Thomas awarded a corner. Zico, the Brazilian player, headed the ball in, but Thomas disallowed the goal, claiming that time was up and he had blown the whistle an instant after the corner kick had been taken. No referee can honestly and realistically say that he can judge when forty-five minutes – allowing time for stoppages – has finished down to a split second. Thomas should have either blown the whistle before the corner was taken or allowed the goal and signalled the end of the match as the players were on the way back to the centre circle for the kick-off.

The man who refereed the 1974 World Cup Final was, of course, Jack Taylor. His performance was brave – he awarded one penalty in the opening minute and another one before half-time – and near faultless. Jack was a superb referee. A game between Leeds United and Arsenal at Elland Road, when Don Revie's team were still at the height of their success, stands out vividly in my mind. Jack was being filmed throughout the whole match. There was a camera trained on him for the entire ninety minutes. When the linesmen entered the dressing room, Jack made us feel very welcome and at ease and said, 'Don't worry about the camera.' He was a quiet and unassuming individual, but had developed a worldwide reputation in football simply because he was such an outstanding referee.

During his pre-match brief, Jack got on to the subject of professionalism in clubs. Jack intimated that he believed Don Revie knew all his strengths and weaknessess as a referee, and he added, 'You'll notice one thing today. If Leeds go a goal ahead, all the ball boys will disappear from around the pitch. It is a little ploy they have at the club which wastes just that extra bit of time. There will then be nobody to retrieve the ball when it goes out of play.'

Jack emphasised how professional clubs had become. Referees must understand that and bear it in mind when making decisions and looking to develop their careers. I ran the line on the side of the main stand, marvelling at the way Jack was controlling affairs. He must have known that the camera was recording his every move, but it did not appear to affect his performance. Jack was the type of referee who was quite prepared to let the game flow. His philosophy was that, if the players wanted to play, he was quite happy to let them do so. He would give and take in terms of decision-making, allowing certain incidents to occur, providing the players acted sensibly. Leeds went a goal ahead and, sure enough, the ball boys disappeared.

I flagged a couple of times within the space of a minute or a minute-and-a-half towards the end of the match. After the final whistle, Jack said to me in the dressing room, 'I thought you were coming into the game a little bit near the end, son. The players wanted to get on with it.' I learned from that.

When I travel into Europe on refereeing appointments, people still talk about Jack Taylor. He is held in enormously high regard. But to me there is one big disappointment. Here is a man who has been right to the top, had refereed in a World Cup Final and, perhaps, twenty-five or thirty different countries, and yet he is almost lost to the game. Sure, he still goes along to the odd society to talk about his experiences, but he has not passed on all the accumulated knowledge to the main hard core of current Football League officals. His expertise has simply not been utilised to the full since he retired. Possibly it is a case of Jack not taking the opportunity to pass on his experience. It might have been a deliberate decision.

One of the greatest thrills of my refereeing career came when I refereed the 1980 FA Cup semi-final at Hillsborough between Liverpool and Arsenal. I then handled the replay at Villa Park. I was naturally a little disappointed that my two-match stint was over and that the tie had still not reached a definite conclusion. I knew the referee had been changed, but I did not know who was doing the third match. I recall switching on the television to watch the highlights and seeing Pat Partridge in the middle. I was thrilled. I suddenly thought that I was performing on the same stage. It was a great compliment that the man who was, at the time, indisputedly the number one referee in England was following me.

Pat was an outstanding referee. Fit, he had a good rapport with players, superb positioning, and was able to get about the play very quickly. He, too, had his fair share of controversial decisions, but he was frequently in the spotlight. One of Pat's idiosyncrasies was that, whenever he cautioned a player, he would bring out his book, place it on his thigh to write a name or comment and always smile. I am sure that smile often took the heat out of a situation. He did not smile by chance. It was something he worked at as he strove to improve his arbitrating. Some people might interpret Pat's smile as his way of showing that he was enjoying taking a player's name, but he had developed such respect among players that they understood his motives and appreciated that he was not gloating.

George McCabe from Sheffield, a 1966 World Cup referee, was a highly respected official. He was something of a hero to me when I first took up the whistle. George still does a lot of voluntary work for youth clubs in and around Sheffield and, even when at the peak of his career, would not be averse to getting out in the parks and passing on advice. You have to admire someone who is prepared to pass on his experiences. George is still involved with the game today, acting as a type of youth liaison officer for Sheffield United, and he certainly nurtures plenty of young footballing talent. As a referee, he was one of the old school, brought up in the days when players respected referees. And George was a good one. In many ways, Jack Taylor, Pat Partridge and George McCabe are three referees on whom I tried most to model my style. I attempted to analyse their particular qualities and strove to get as close as possible to an amalgam of those qualities.

Gordon Hill was regarded as the players' referee. I ran the line for him and, at times, I could hear Gordon using the occasional slice of bad language. A few 'ifs' and 'buts'! This allowed Gordon to relate to players – they often considered him as 'one of the lads' – and he had a very relaxed manner. Personally, I never use bad language on the pitch. I think it is important for referees to treat players and the match itself with respect.

Of the current referees, none has done more to improve links between officials and players over the last two or three years than Neil Midgley. Neil is something of an unsung hero. While other referees receive more publicity and plaudits, Neil is flogging his guts out to bring players closer to referees. He has the superb knack of communicating with a smile on the pitch, and off it he is regularly attending dinners, seminars and the like, talking to players and trying to prove that referees are only human. He tells a good story and enjoys a joke, but at the same time is both sensible and accurate in his approach to the laws.

George Courtney, a highly capable official and a man much respected in his handling of matches, is a rival of mine. He was appointed the English referee for the 1984 European Championships – with me as his senior linesman. I make no secret of the fact that I would have liked it to have been the other way round, but George is that much more experienced than me – he is some years older and has been a Football League referee for rather longer. I would like to think that we will both be in contention for selection for the 1986 World Cup Finals. Perhaps we might both go to Mexico, maybe one of us will be disappointed. There is certainly great competition and rivalry among referees to be appointed for the top games and tournaments.

The match the English 'team' of officials (George, myself and Keith Miller) took in the European Championships was the semi-final between Spain and Denmark at Lyon. George had a very busy time cautioning eight players and then sending off Berggren of Denmark for a second yellow-card offence. George had been told before the match to maintain a firm grip and that he certainly did.

I was pleased that John Hunting of Leicester was appointed referee for the 1984 FA Cup Final – it was the fitting end to the career of a man who, at the time of his retirement, had been on the FIFA panel longer than any other English referee, and he was the only FIFA referee who had not handled the Cup Final.

Referees, even those at the top of the Football League, are always developing their careers. An official can never stop learning. When a referee first gets elevated to the Football League, he is one of the new boys. He needs to get established. You do not get a good reputation in a couple of seasons. It is when a referee begins to visit clubs more than once that word of his ability begins to get around. One decent performance at a club can be dismissed as a 'flash in the pan'. Two or more good matches is no coincidence.

There is an old saying that, if you are known to be a good referee, you start off with ten marks and they are deducted in people's minds if you make errors. A new referee, though, begins with nought and must gain his marks and work hard for every one. There is some truth in that. At the same time, no referee must ever become complacent. Every official, no matter who he is, goes through a bad patch, when things simply refuse to work out how he would wish. It might well be at the semi-final stage of a competition when, with a great game anticipated, nerves take over and the players do not produce their true form. A referee might become caught up in the general level of mediocrity. He will need to make certain tolerances, bearing in mind the importance of the occasion. Possibly one side is three goals adrift with just ten minutes remaining of an important match. Frustrations are bound to creep in. The same applies to a local derby match or a dull goalless draw, when the the referee must be particularly alert. A section of the game that is uninteresting is a sure breeding ground for a flashpoint. Or, if the referee makes a mistake in the last minute of a hitherto uneventful match, he is bound to become the focus of attention. The same error during a six-goal thriller might pass virtually unnoticed.

That FA Cup semi-final between Liverpool and Arsenal in 1980 was my first really big match, although I had already done a League Cup semi-final. Arsenal eventually triumphed after a four-match marathon, before losing 1-0 to West Ham in the Final itself. The first semi-final at Hillsborough was just round the corner from where I lived. It was so close, in fact, that I had lunch at home and walked to the ground. Consequently, I was able to submit a 'nil' expenses claim – which, I understand, pleasantly staggered the FA officials at Lancaster Gate! I was paid the princely sum of £35, but I would have gladly done the match for nothing. I do not think that at any stage of a referee's career, money should be a consideration. People tell me that I am on an ego trip, but it is not that, either. It is simply a case of that, when I was a teenager, I took up a hobby – refereeing – and, being an ambitious sort of person, I wanted to be good at it and progress as far as possible. The whole thing has snowballed. I remember, very early in my career, the first time I went outside the Sheffield area to handle a match. I picked up the Yorkshire League fixture list one day and saw that I was due to run the line in the match between Bridlington Trinity and Bridlington Town. 'Crikey,' I thought, 'I'm going to Bridlington. That means I'll be away from home for an entire day for a single match.' I went to the game with Eric Loukes, a Football League linesman at the time, and Alan Burgin. I got as much pleasure out of that as I do now refereeing a match at Anfield.

By the 1984-85 season, the fee for refereeing Football League and FA Cup matches had gone up to £43, plus travelling expenses and an overnight stay at a local hotel, if necessary. But, if anything, I lose money by handling matches, bearing in mind the amount of time it occupies, and I believe it is right that we do not make money. The last thing football wants is to attract the wrong type of person into refereeing – the mercenaries.

People often say to me, 'I saw you on the box last night. I understand the top players are earning £500 or even £1000 a week. You can't be on a bad whack for a game yourself.'

'Forty-three quid.'

'You must be bloody mad.'

The game is a hobby – a love – but I must adopt a professional attitude. I would never want to give it up before my time. But if tomorrow I received a letter from the Football Association saying they had decided that, in future, all referees operating at the highest club level would be full-time professionals and the salary they were offering was, say, £8000 a year, would I be interested? As much as it would hurt, I would have to be realistic. As a sales director, I am not earning a bad wage and I have a wife, a family and a mortgage. To suddenly accept a lower standard of living would make me a loser, and that is not my scene. If, however, the salary offered by the FA was £25,000 per annum, or a figure with which I could pretty much maintain my current standard of living, I would give it careful consideration. I would, however, have to ask myself what I would do after my refereeing days are over.

I would hate to see the situation where people are attracted into refereeing for any reason other than their love of it. It is not really possible, either, to play one day and referee the next. Players tend to watch the ball, referees should usually keep their eyes on the players. The ball, a round object that bounces about and might perform certain tricks in the wind, never commits a foul. The discipline required to watch the players and not the ball comes with experience. Referees should also not be pushed through the ranks too quickly. It is a recipe for calamity to give a young referee a big match before he has acquired the necessary experience.

I remember when I had been refereeing for about seven years, many people in Sheffield were telling me that I would make it right to the top. My attitude and performance was just right, they said. Soon I started to get itchy feet. When the invitation to join the Football League list did not come, I became frustrated, and even more so when the letter did not arrive the following season – or the next, or the next. I felt I was being rejected, and it was difficult to accept at the time. Looking back, I was probably not even considered. I had to grit my teeth and say to myself, 'I am going to make it. I'm just going to have to wait another year or two.' In retrospect, I am sure it was a blessing that I was not selected for the Football League list at that stage. I would probably have been scrubbed off by now because the standard of my performance would simply not have been up to scratch.

I recall refereeing a Northern Premier League match and being quite content with my performance. I was looking forward to receiving the assessor's report, which on this occasion was compiled by a gentleman called Maurice O'Brien from Bolton. When the letter arrived in the morning, my eldest son Paul brought it up to my bedroom and I asked him to read it out aloud. I was stunned. I thought Maurice was talking a load of nonsense. He was, in effect, telling me that I could not referee, and all because I had been running with the whistle in my mouth. It was a sure sign that I was blowing my whistle too readily, he told me, and, what is more, I would one day be struck by the ball in the mouth. Sure enough, it happened shortly afterwards.

Initially, that type of report created an adverse reaction. There is a danger that referees make radical changes to their style and, in the next assessment, are told they have over-compensated. After being told that you are not taking a firm enough line, you should not go out and send off three or four players in the following match. You must accept that the assessor's views are merely an opinion and you can either accept or reject them. If you can be objective about your performance – in the way that the assessor has been – you will surely improve as an official.

I am a strong believer in the assessor system. When I was a young referee right at the start of my career, I had to go and ask lots of questions about how I had performed. Nowadays, each Football League match is watched by an independent observer – often a former referee – and his report is sent to the match referee and written in the second person. For example, it might say, 'You did not give sufficiently clear signals,' or 'The co-operation between you and your linesmen broke down when they spotted an off-the-ball incident, but you did not consult them.' I have kept every assessment I have ever received on the Football League and now have a pile about six inches high. I regularly refer to them, reading and re-reading them in batches and looking for trends. The assessor, who is studying every aspect of the referee's performance, gives you a mark out of ten and also sends a copy of his report to the Football League or Football Association.

II
Referee-Linesman Co-operation

Anybody who referees in the local park or recreation ground will tell you that twenty-two players take a bit of handling. They are niggling at each other, and often at the referee himself. The man in the middle has to make instant decisions on his own and then take the consequences. But, if a referee progresses, perhaps doing a semi-final or final of a local cup for the first time, he will have two linesmen to help him. He might be in for a shock.

Suddenly, the referee is not just looking after twenty-two players, but two colleagues as well. A poor linesman is more of a hindrance than a help. Somebody who waves his flag wildly or unnecessarily or a linesman who simply does not understand the laws and their interpretation is a waste of time. Nevertheless, even only a moderately competent linesman can be used to advantage. One of the secrets of a good referee is the man able to utilise his linesmen to his advantage. It is all a question of one of the most important facets of officiating – referee-linesman co-operation.

Three officials, working efficiently as a team and with confidence in each other, help appease players, managers and spectators alike. The result is simple – a better match.

A linesman is not just the fellow who waves his flag when the ball goes out of play. He provides another pair of eyes for the referee, plays a significant part in maintaining control and often makes crucial decisions. Taken to its conclusion, a decision made by a linesman could alter the destiny of the World Cup Final. Because, if the referee has faith in his linesman, he will accept his decision and act on it.

I was provided with a graphic illustration of the need for referees to take note of their linesmen early in my career. Great Harwood were playing Hyde United in the Northern Premier League and I was running the line. I remember feeling somewhat awe-inspired walking out onto the field because the Great Harwood team included such renowned former professionals as Bryan Douglas and Ronnie Clayton, both outstanding players with Blackburn and England, and Adam Blacklaw, the Scottish international goalkeeper, who played for Burnley and Blackburn. This was fairly typical for teams at this level, which comprised largely a mixture of men who had played at the top, coming gracefully towards the end of their careers, and youngsters progressing in the game and determined to reach the Football League. Sometimes the mixture did not gell.

A Football League linesman was refereeing this match at Hyde. I could almost touch Bryan Douglas from the line. He was playing superbly, totally tying up his opposing full back, who was being made to look a bit of a fool by Douglas' skill. Then, midway through the first half, the young full back clearly decided the only way to stop Douglas was by illicit means – kicking hell out of him. Douglas was sent sprawling by a clumsy foul but, after treatment, was able to continue. Despite my flagging vigorously, the referee took no notice of me. A few minutes later, Douglas was kicked even more violently. Again he continued and again the referee ignored me, the linesman. After the third foul, Douglas decided he had had enough and limped back to the dressing room. The referee took no action against the young full back and neither consulted me nor acknowledged my flag-waving. It was a classic example of poor referee-linesman co-operation.

Mind you, I was once embarrassed by acting upon a linesman waving his flag. It happened when I was appointed to referee a Division Two match in the Sheffield County Senior League at Hallam, another Yorkshire ground with a huge slope, not dissimilar to that at Yeovil. The League provided no linesmen which, especially on this large, sloping pitch, made offsides difficult to spot. The referee was expected to keep up with play as best as possible and I was preparing myself for an exhausting match. Then salvation.

A man knocked on the dressing room door and volunteered to run the line. He told me he had been operating as a class three referee for a couple of years. Naturally, I was delighted. He seemed fully genned up on the laws, so I happily gave him authority to perform all the duties of linesman, including, of course, flagging for offsides. In the opening minutes, he gave two or three offside decisions – which I checked by running opposite him – and his judgement was spot on. He clearly knew his stuff and I looked forward to an easier afternoon than usual with what was a rare privilege in those days – one linesman, if not a pair.

After about fifteen minutes, my expert linesman suddenly began waving his flag. I blew my whistle and stopped the game, wondering what was wrong because no player could conceivably be offside. Perhaps there had been a skirmish off the ball? I ran over and enquired what the problem was. 'Doesn't matter, ref,' he replied enthusiastically, 'I'm just waving my flag because my mate's coming in the top gate and I want him to know that I'm running the line.' Red-faced, I re-started the match with a drop ball among laughing players.

The best way for officials to improve their co-operation with each other is by handling as many matches as possible. FIFA decided that teams of three officials from fourteen countries would officiate in the 1984 European Championship in France. The idea was that the men would then become familiar with each other's style and there would be no language problems between the officials. This, of course, made complete sense and the team of officials from England had three games together in English domestic soccer prior to travelling. The team was George Courtney as referee, myself as senior linesman and Keith Miller as the other linesman.

I have always maintained that it is important for a referee to keep his hand in at running the line. As a FIFA referee, I might be called on at any time to act as a linesman. I often volunteer my services to run the line in a park match. On a number of occasions, I have taken the flag in the Ford Motor Company's inter-departmental competition at Dagenham. Both players and spectators have told me that they find it strange that an international referee should officiate at this more modest level, but I believe no official can have too much exposure to match situations. All experience is good experience and, ultimately, effort will be rewarded.

People say to me, 'How is it that one week you can be refereeing at Old Trafford or Highbury and next week doing a match involving amateurs?' I remember after doing one of my first matches at Anfield, I received a call from a reporter on the *Liverpool Echo* and he asked me where my next appointment was.

'Concord Park,' I replied.

'Where?'

'Concord Park in Sheffield. I've been doing matches there ever since I started refereeing,' I told him. 'We're lucky now because there are showers. For years, players from more than twenty pitches changed in one communal dressing room.'

I know some referees disagree with me, but I would much rather be out on a Saturday afternoon refereeing a match than doing nothing. So, if I do not have a Football League appointment, I will usually attempt to pick up a match from somewhere.

Some of those participating in the local park try to get themselves cautioned on purpose, so they can go into the pub after the game and say, 'I've been booked by a bloke who's reffed the Cup Final,' or 'Keith Hackett's just taken my name.' The overall attitude, though, of amateur and professional players is the same – both want to win. Over the years, I have seen the standard of fitness among players in junior football improve dramatically and nowadays there is a tendency towards Sunday football rather than Saturdays.

This chapter is designed to provide an insight into ways of improving referee-linesman co-operation. It describes the measures I take to ensure the officals perform capably as a team in Football League matches. Most of these procedures can also apply to matches at lower levels.

Before the match The most important time in improving co-operation between the referee and his linesmen is before the ball has even been kicked. It is crucial the officials arrive well in advance of kick-off. For

Football League matches, this would be around one o'clock for a three o'clock start. This might be a little early for games in lower leagues, but it is still vital that the referee and linesmen arrive in plenty of time to discuss tactics and sort out any problems.

Many things help to add to the performance of a linesman and the improvement of his co-operation with the referee. His appearance – both when he arrives at the ground and during the match itself – should be immaculate. Collar and tie are the order of the day. I have seen some amazingly foolish and sloppy habits practised by some linesmen. Smoking before the match must always hint at lack of fitness and concern. It is not unknown for linesmen to ask some of the players for their autographs, but I think that any sign of being overawed is a sure way of losing a player's respect and confidence. Perhaps worst of all, I have even seen a linesman arrive at the ground with his young son bedecked in the home team's colours.

In the period before the match, the referee can get to know his linesmen and explain what he requires of them. One of them will be the senior linesman, who will take over from the referee if he sustains an injury or is unable to continue for any other reason. One of the first things I do, especially at a big match, is to take my two linesmen onto the pitch. This is of paramount importance at the more imposing grounds such as Anfield, Old Trafford, Highbury and White Hart Lane. This relaxed walkabout helps the officials to become acclimatised to the atmosphere, and to avoid being surprised and unsettled by the tumult that awaits them when they walk out for the match itself. We also do a physical inspection of the pitch, goals and parts of the stadium.

We check the pitch markings and the ground itself. There might be a little surface water or frost on the grass. If this is discovered early enough, there is sufficient time for the groundsman to do something about it. We check that the nets are firmly secured to the post and ground, because it is not unknown for the ball to go straight through a net. It is also important to look at the environment of the pitch. The flag, a small piece of material, admittedly bright in colour, can sometimes be difficult to see – especially in an evening match at a ground where the floodlighting is dim. There are a number of grounds on the Football League where the linesman with the red flag would never run the line in front of the main stand. One example is Wolverhampton Wanderers. The seats in the old stand at Molineux are red and, when the crowd is sparsely sprinkled among the seats, a red flag blends into the background. It is extremely difficult to notice at a glance, so it is important to look at the background of the area surrounding the pitch and decide which colour flag will be used on which side. While I was in America, I had to use two yellow flags at one match because the cheerleaders standing near the touchline were waving red flags.

An official from the home club should also be consulted to ensure that if the ball boys are being used, they do not wear tracksuits that clash with the shirts of either team, or that the boys are not going to be positioned where they might obscure the linesmen's view of proceedings. I usually then take a walk outside the ground or have a quick look at anything of local interest. I am always pleased if my linesmen come with me – it all helps to build up a rapport.

With an hour or so to go before kick-off, I settle in my dressing room and commence a slow change. I don't like a rush. That is why I lay out all my kit when I first arrive. I want to make certain it is complete – especially my footwear. Blisters are a recipe for disaster. I also advise my linesmen to lay out their kit on arrival.

Around half an hour before the start, the team captains and managers or other club officials bring their teamsheets into the dressing room. One important point here is to ensure that the goalkeepers' jerseys do not clash with the opposing team's colours. I have seen matches when a goalkeeper, wearing green, runs onto the pitch only to discover that the opposition's shirts are also green.

These days the rules do not stipulate that boots have to be checked. Nevertheless, before big matches, I sometimes ask my linesmen to check players' studs at random. In continental matches, anything from thirty minutes to an hour before kick-off, the referee and linesmen will inspect studs. Then, in the tunnel area just before emerging onto the pitch, the linesmen will make another cursory inspection.

Twenty minutes to go and the most crucial time of all for ensuring proper referee-linesman co-operation. My pep talk. I must make certain that my linesmen understand fully what I require of them. They are there to assist, but it is no good their not knowing how they can help, so I will ask them to sit down and attempt to grasp their attention. My pre-match talk might begin something like this. . . .

'I am the referee and you are the linesmen, but don't think of it like that. We are three referees. Our job is to control this match and we're going to do it by working as a team. We want to be seen as efficient, firm, fair and in control at all times.

'If the players want to play football, then we are going to let them. We are going to interfere only as and when necessary. Please remember that I'm a referee who likes to play a fairly high level of advantage and keep the game flowing as much as possible. This enhances spectator enjoyment. So recognise that. Don't continue flagging when it is clear I have played an advantage. Maintain eye-to-eye contact and look before you take action.

'Obviously, I want you to run in the outside right position. That means I run from corner to corner and, while doing that, must keep the ball between myself and you, the linesmen, so that we're in vision at all times. It is not always easy to achieve, but is what we must aim for.

'When you raise your flag, which is your means of communication with me, it is vital to do so in an accurate manner and in a way that I can see easily. The arm – with the flag at the end of it – must be raised at forty-five degrees. Not sixty, not seventy, but forty-five. You should always face the field of play and be prepared to change the flag from one hand to the other. I don't want a flag held in the right hand signalling a throw, with your arm stretched across your face.

'I want all loose balls chased, apart from when you are standing still signalling for offside. So, if there is a back pass from a defender or the ball is rolling gently towards the goalkeeper, don't assume it is going to be safely gathered. Maybe in one out of one hundred occasions, it could roll into the goal, get stuck in the mud or the 'keeper might fumble the ball and it goes for a corner. And you can bet that the time you don't follow the ball, that is when it happens. I want you to be in line to check whether the ball crosses the goal line.'

I will then explain the role I expect the linesmen to adopt in every conceivable match situation. I try not to preach; merely attempt to stress the type of things I expect. Remember, each referee has his own idiosyncrasies and the linesmen might not be familiar with mine. So, if necessary, I demonstrate what my own signals mean.

If the match is important – perhaps a First Division game or cup tie – I try to relax my colleagues. I tell them it is just another game, no different really from the one in the park. Conversely, it is sometimes necessary to motivate the linesmen before a lower division fixture with no apparent significance. I'm always striving to get a high level of performance.

I recall doing an international match abroad in 1983. My colleagues were Ken Bissix of Bath, who was in his last season as a Football League linesman, and Ken Salmon from Barnet, the League referee and a man with a particularly dry sense of humour. We were not exactly on edge, but were mentally prepared for the big match and we helped relieve the tension by sharing a joke at Ken Bissix's expense.

We pulled our socks from our bags to lay them out. Both mine and Ken Salmon's were the type with three white hoops at the top, while Ken Bissix's were black with just a plain white turnover. Salmon pointed out that it was vital we all looked the same, and that Bissix really would have to do something about it. Fortunately, said Salmon, he had some black boot polish with him, which could be applied to the white turnover to simulate hoops. At a distance, nobody would know the difference. When Salmon asked Bissix to remove his socks to perform his masterpiece of art, he duly obliged. Myself and Ken Salmon could conceal our mirth no longer. We burst into laughter. Ken Bissix took the joke in the right spirit and the incident helped us to relax and, I'm sure, improved our performance as a result.

After talking with my colleagues and trying to develop understanding and sympathy, thus avoiding the situation where I give the decision one way and the linesman gives it the other, we do a quick final check on equipment. Have the linesmen got their watches and notebooks and, in the case of the senior linesman, a whistle? Or even their flags? Then we prepare to go out on the pitch, but there is still more co-operation required before the game begins.

The introductions to the two captains must be conducted in a formal manner. I stress that. I do not want one of the linesmen wandering about fifteen yards away from the centre-spot to greet and shake one of the captains' hands. They might be best of friends or next-door neighbours, but it gives the impression that that linesman might just favour that player's team. I am utterly convinced that all Football League officials are unbiased, but you try telling that to the fans of the other team. I insist my linesmen remain within close proximity during the introductions. They then move away quickly to check the nets again. The match can then begin and I hope the linesmen have remembered all I have told them.

Offside Offside decisions form the major task of linesmen, and from my experience of running the line I know it is not an easy job. Linesmen must stay in line with the second rear-most defender at all times. He must be level with the player. So, when the defender moves a yard either way, so does the linesman. It is no good being five yards in front or five yards behind. The best – indeed the only – way to judge a close offside is to be level with the second rear-most defender, in which case the linesman's decision is less likely to be questioned by players.

If a linesman sees a player in an offside position, he must then ask himself if he is interfering with play and seeking to gain advantage. A good linesman will develop the ability to slightly delay waving his flag. This allows him to read the situation before committing himself to a decision. Sometimes, when looking at a game from a side-on position, the ball can be booted downfield and it looks as though it is going to land on, say, the right wing. A linesman, spotting a player on that side of the pitch in an offside position, raises his flag, but falls victim to the optical illusion. In the event, the ball drops on the other side of the pitch and the right-winger clearly is not interfering with play. The linesman will feel something of a chump for flagging, so the good linesman will wait that extra split-second to make certain where the ball is going to land.

If the linesman has signalled for offside, but I believe the ball is travelling safely to a defender or the goalkeeper, I might wave play on. In that situation, it is important to acknowledge the linesman's signal. A simple gesture of thanks will increase the referee's popularity with his colleagues.

Penalties If the referee is several yards adrift of the play when a player is brought down near the edge of the penalty area, he is in no position to judge whether the offence took place inside the box. This is where the linesman comes in. He first indicates that the foul has taken place and then, if appropriate, holds his flag across his chest to show the infringement was inside the penalty area. The same applies to handballs.

A penalty is obviously one of the most significant decisions a referee can make, but, unless he has clearly made an error, it is important to accept the linesman's judgement. A correctly-positioned linesman is better-placed than a referee on the halfway line to assess the exact location of the offence. To go against him is to undermine a linesman's judgement and credibility. The referee will consequently lose the linesman's support and, quite likely, receive an inferior service.

Once a penalty kick has been awarded, I ask my linesman to stand on the goal line, ten yards from each upright *(See Diagram 3)*. I watch for

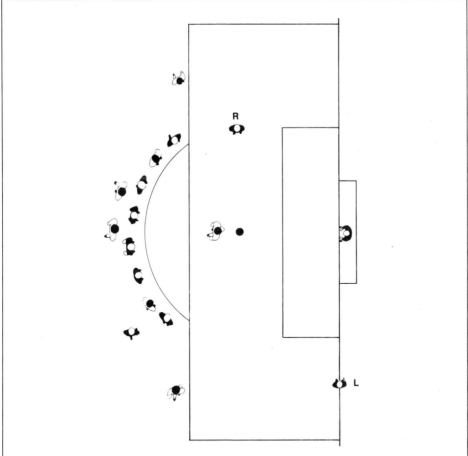

Diagram 3 *Penalties* The referee (R) watches for encroachment by attacking and defending players and for any movement by the goalkeeper while the linesman (L) checks that the ball crosses the goal line

encroachment and the goalkeeper moving early, while the linesman's sole duty is to determine whether or not the ball crosses the line. He is then in the best position if, for example, a 1966 World Cup Final situation arises. Then, a shot from Geoff Hurst, not from a penalty, struck the underside of the crossbar and bounced down onto the line. Nobody has ever discovered categorically whether the ball crossed the line. In another instance, the goalkeeper might partially save the ball. Again the linesman is ideally placed to decide whether the ball creeps over the line.

Corners Linesmen indicate corners by pointing their own flag at the corner flag. Once the kick has been awarded, I ask the linesman to occupy a position ten yards from the corner flag on the goal line if the kick is to be taken on his side of the pitch. This enables him to prevent opposing players encroaching to within less than ten yards. The linesman must stop players short, maybe twelve or thirteen yards from the flag, rather than allow them to get close and then be faced with the difficult task of making them retreat to ten yards. In European or FIFA matches, I do not want my linesmen to stand on the goal line, but as close as possible to the corner flag without obstructing the kicker. This is because UEFA and FIFA prefer that linesmen do not enter the field of play and, therefore, cut the corners of the pitch when hurrying back to their position on the touchline. Once the linesman has ensured the ball is placed in the quadrant, I can signal for the corner to be taken.

Free kicks I will have stressed to my linesmen my desire to play advantage as frequently as possible. Therefore, it is important that the linesmen do not keep waving their flags too hastily and ruin the opportunity to keep the game flowing. This applies to fouls, handballs and offsides.

The two imaginary rectangles formed by the penalty area line and touchline, and goal area line and penalty area line are regions of the pitch I expect the linesmen to keep a particularly close eye on for free kick infringements. Indeed, I would go as far as to say that the linesmen should 'referee' these areas. Not if I am standing next to the play, but if I have been caught some distance from the ball by a sudden long pass. The linesman is close enough to make a judgement and if I, acting upon his decision, blow for a free kick, possible retaliation might be avoided.

Throw-ins If the ball goes out of play in the first eighteen yards of each end of the pitch – in other words, in line with either penalty area – I expect my linesmen to indicate to the player exactly where the throw is to be taken.

This can be done simply by talking to the player. When the throw-in is between either penalty area, I will move to opposite the point where it is to be taken, about twenty yards in from the touchline. If a player attempts to gain ground by taking the throw from the wrong place, three short blasts on the whistle and a signal to get him in line with me usually does the trick. If the linesman is not sure which way a throw-in should be awarded, he will raise his flag directly above his head and the referee will then indicate the direction.

Goal kicks Linesmen should check that goal kicks are taken within the goal (six yard) area and then run to the edge of the penalty area to check that the kick goes out of the box *(See Diagram 4)*. At punted clearances, the linesman must watch that the goalkeeper does not handle the ball outside the penalty area. The linesman must then sprint upfield to take up his position in line with the second rear-most defender. Linesmen, as well as referees, need to do a lot of running during a match and should have worked up quite a sweat at the end of ninety minutes.

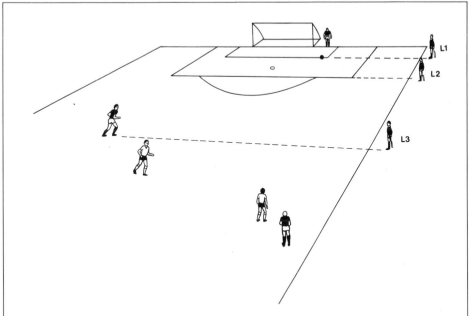

Diagram 4 *Goal kicks*   The linesman first checks that the ball is correctly positioned (L1), then moves to observe the ball leaving the penalty area (L2) and finally takes up his regular offside position (L3)

Behind my back It is not possible for a referee to watch all of the players all of the time. So it is up to the linesmen to keep an eye on what is happening behind my back and to provide two further pairs of eyes. It could be that play has developed from close-to to a linesman with a long ball upfield and two players become involved in a fracas on my blind side. It is then that I want him to act. Maybe a word or a shout will be sufficient to diffuse the situation, or the linesman might have to draw my attention to it.

Stoppages and flare-ups Linesmen must not relax when the game has stopped, perhaps because of injury to a player. They must go on a red alert, watching for possible flare-ups and incidents away from the centre of attention – the injured player.

If I feel I need assistance to deal with a flare-up that may occur either during play or while the game has been stopped, I divide the pitch into two halves lengthways. An official is not under any circumstances allowed to strike a player, but my size usually enables me to assert myself. The linesman on the side of the trouble should come onto the pitch to help me separate the players, while the other linesman remains on the line writing in his notebook the identity of those players inciting the trouble. Once the situation has calmed, I can then consult him and take the necessary action. I never like to have both linesmen on the pitch at the same time, because if all three officials are involved, they might have distorted views of the incident and the real offenders could escape unpunished.

The dug-out The dug-out, or simply the point from which the manager, coach, substitute and so on watch the match, is usually on the side of the pitch run by the senior linesman. I ask my linesmen not to look for trouble in this area, which does not mean they have to opt out, but simply deal with any problems in an orderly manner, employing commonsense. I do not expect a linesman to leave his line and poke his head in the box, shouting and bawling at the manager or trainer. A look, or a quite word, is normally sufficient, because an officious approach often inflames the situation and creates further problems for the referee, who already has enough to deal with on the pitch.

I recall a match some years ago at Bury, when Colin Seel was refereeing and I was running the line. Everything had been progressing smoothly with Colin handling affairs expertly. Then he awarded a corner kick. The linesman on the opposite side of the pitch to me was supervising the ball when, just as the kick was about to be taken, a substitution was made. Colin ran over to check the on-coming player's studs. But suddenly another player was lying flat on the floor, apparently having been struck by a member of the opposition. Colin immediately looked towards his two linesmen to discover what had happened, but we had let him down. Our attention had been distracted by the substitution and we had missed the incident. It taught me an important lesson. When I was running the line, I would, in future, pay particular attention when the referee's view of the players was temporarily diverted.

I also decided that, when I was refereeing, I would not check the studs of an on-coming player, but ask my senior linesman to do so. I could, therefore, keep an eye on the remaining players. Now I ask my linesmen to make sure the player does not come on until the man he is replacing has left the pitch and that the substitution takes place on the halfway line. It might sound finicky, but a uniformity of action alleviates problems. The linesmen must also record the time of any substitutions. I never do this, getting out my notebook only when I am cautioning or sending-off a player. It I start writing when a substitution is made, the crowd and other players might think I am taking a player's name.

Time Linesmen, as well as the referee, carry a watch and it is their duty to indicate to the referee how much time is remaining. With five minutes to go before half-time and full-time, the linesmen should place the flat of their hands against their shorts and, when the forty-five minutes of each half are up on their watches, put their free arm across their chest. The referee must acknowledge these signals, although he might add some time for injuries and stoppages. The referee must always look for the linesmen's signals because, even though he carries two watches, he could misread his watch or one of them could be faulty. More than once, a referee has blown his whistle a few minutes early.

I do not want my linesmen fussing to find out how many sugars Joe Bloggs wants in his tea at half-time. The ten-minute inverval is a time for analysis and discussion. How has the first half gone? Are there any areas in which we are not performing well? Have I missed a linesman's flag at any time? Can they hear my whistle? We should be searching for points that will help improve our performance in the second half. We must not fall into the trap of complacency if somebody says, 'Ref and linesmen, you've had a terrific first-half.' We all enjoy congratulation, but it is hopeless if we make a mess of things after the re-start.

After the match The linesmen should keep the players in view when they are leaving the field and join the referee as quickly as possible just in case there is a flare-up, or a player or manager is protesting. I ask my linesmen not to say anything as they leave the pitch. One might comment, 'Well done, ref, you had a great game' within earshot of a player who has been a nuisance throughout the match. Perhaps I have cautioned him or awarded a penalty against him and, on hearing the linesman praise the referee, suddenly cracks, hurling a torrent of abuse. I would then have to report him to the Football Association for foul and abusive language – something I never enjoy doing.

A manager might be enraged by a decision given by either the referee or linesman that has, in his eyes, cost his team the match. I tell my colleagues to avoid a manager who is clearly het up and intent on verbally attacking an official. That does not mean run round corners and hide, but merely avoid getting drawn into a conversation that will eventually become an argument. A polite, 'Sorry, I've no comment' and into the dressing room is a more tactful policy than becoming involved in what could develop into a major problem.

Once we are all in the dressing room, it is not simply a case of getting changed and going home. Honest, constructive criticism on each other's performance will help us do better in the next game.

Appointments abroad Referee-linesman co-operation is never stronger than when covering matches overseas. When I am doing a game in Europe, my linesmen are usually both from England. We spend two or three days together, providing an opportunity for familiarity with each other's personality and officiating technique, with an improved performance the hopeful outcome.

Myself and the two linesmen congregate at a London hotel on the Monday evening for a Wednesday match. We ensure our passports, clothing, kit and so on are in order, and our flight tickets and, if necessary, visas have been obtained by the FA. One or other of the linesmen might have asked for advice about how much luggage he should take. My advice is always to travel light. I will take the blazer and grey flannels provided by the FA to FIFA referees, a sweater, three shirts, a pair of slacks, track suit and my kit. I will put it all in one bag and always attempt to take it as hand luggage to avoid possible delays at baggage claim areas, or even lost baggage. I do not want my boots in transit when I am supposed to be refereeing a match. I travelled to one European match with a linesman who had never flown before. As the aircraft was taxiing down the runway, his knuckles were white with fear. He needed plenty of reassurance before eventually relaxing and enjoying the journey.

We are usually met by officials of either the club or the country we are visiting. They will assist us through customs and passport control and drive us to our hotel. Occasionally, we might be invited to attend a banquet – which can be quite lavish affairs – on the Tuesday evening prior to the match and, of course, we monitor carefully our intake of food and alchohol. More often than not, though, we are taken to a local restaurant.

The following morning, around ten o'clock, my two colleagues and I visit the ground to inspect the pitch, dressing rooms and stadium itself, to familiarise ourselves with the match surroundings and check that there are no problems. If the match kicks off in the afternoon, we usually go for a quick drive around the town; an evening start allows us time to sightsee on foot. I ensure myself and the two linesmen have a lengthy rest period. For me, that means a lie on the bed while reading. I will have, perhaps, a cup of tea and a couple of sandwiches before arriving at the ground at least an hour and a half before kick-off. We meet the UEFA observer, a high-powered official there to report on the match itself and the conduct of players, officials and spectators. We ensure the captains sign their team sheets and take the names of the five officials allowed on the bench, together with their titles. The man in charge of the bench should also sign the documents. I warn my linesmen of the different environment they can expect at foreign matches – thundercrackers, rockets and smoke bombs let off by the volatile spectators provide a lively and exciting scenario to games abroad. I am always proud to represent England as referee in charge of international matches and it should provide the ultimate incentive to any prospective or current referee to work at his game.

After the game, we chat, have a few drinks and eat a meal. An early departure on Thursday morning means we normally arrive back in England before lunchtime. What I expect of the linesmen in the game itself varies little from the Football League. The language barrier is overcome by gesticulating and facial expressions. I will give the linesmen my usual talk before the match in an effort to foster that most important facet in the smooth running of any soccer match: referee-linesman co-operation.

European countries leave Britain behind in the way they give young referees the opportunity to handle matches in front of huge crowds. Before some European matches, a junior game will be played as a type of curtain-raiser. This will be refereed by a boy of, maybe, eighteen. What an experience for him. I saw this prior to the European Championship semi-final at Lyon and also before Inter Milan's game against Hamburg in the 1984-85 UEFA Cup. It would be marvellous if British referees could have similar experiences.

12

Penalty, Ref!

No refereeing decision causes greater controversy or debate than the awarding of a penalty. The reason is simple. A penalty more often than not leads to a goal and, therefore, is frequently vital to the destiny of a match. A footballer, aiming for a target of eight yards by eight feet from a distance of twelve yards, and with his path blocked only by the opposing goalkeeper, should always expect to score. And he usually does.

Consequently, it is crucial the referee does not make an error in his decision to give the penalty and, once the kick has been awarded, that he deals capably with often angry and frustrated players and makes sure the kick is conducted within the laws. There are nine infringements for which, if they take place in the penalty area and are committed intentionally by a defender, a penalty should be awarded. They are:

(a) If a player kicks or attempts to kick an opponent.

(b) If a player trips an opponent, i.e. throwing or attempting to throw him by the use of the legs or by stooping in front of or behind him.

(c) If a player jumps at an opponent.

(d) If a player charges an opponent in a violent or dangerous manner.

(e) If a player charges an opponent from behind unless the latter be obstructing.

(f) If a player strikes or attempts to strike an opponent.

(g) If a player holds an opponent.

(h) If a player pushes an opponent.

(i) If a player handles the ball, i.e. carries, strikes or propels the ball with his hand or arm. (This does not apply to the goalkeeper within his own penalty area).

It is important that the referee and linesmen are in the correct position to spot any of these nine offences. An attacking side will become just as irate if they are not awarded what they believe should be a penalty, as will a defending team who concede what they consider to be a harsh penalty. In all cases, even when the ball is nowhere near the eighteen-yard area, the ideal position for the officials to watch for infringements is for the ball to remain between the referee and linesmen.

Once the referee has decided to award a penalty, he should make his intentions clear in a firm and positive manner. The referee should point to the penalty mark, but that is all. (Incidentally, it is often called the penalty spot. This is particular anathema to me. The point from where the penalty is taken does not have to be a spot; it could quite easily be a cross.) Those referees who first point to the mark, run towards it and then stand over it are inviting problems. I have done it in the past and experience has shown me that I am running right into the area of greatest and most concentrated player dissent. There is often a large proportion of one team wanting to dispute the decision. The referee, by standing over the penalty mark and pointing to it, is in effect defying anybody to challenge his decision, and that is just what the players will do. The best procedure is to point to the penalty mark, perhaps run towards it for a pace or two and then move away from the mark and in the direction of where you are going to stand to supervise the kick. The referee can still expect a great deal of dissent, but some of the players will feel that nothing is to be gained from chasing the referee half the width of the pitch.

The players disputing the decision often do so not because they actually believe the referee has made a mistake or that he will reverse his decision, but because the extra little slice of time that their protestations cause to elapse will increase the pressure on the kicker. It is a piece of gamesmanship. It is imperative the referee takes a firm line and controls the situation effectively. To do this, it might be necessary to caution one or more players.

The referee can often be faced with a posse of players disputing his decision and he must decide which one or ones he should caution. One trick that I have used quite successfully in the past is to walk a few further paces backwards. If, for example, five players have been disputing, often one of them will continue forward, still exchanging words, while the remaining four will abandon their torrent of dissent. The player who continues can be cautioned, but the referee must apply commonsense and not decide to caution huge numbers of players whenever they show the slightest disappointment at the decision to award a penalty. Even if it is the most clear-cut penalty of all time, players are still bound to be a little frustrated.

The referee can sometimes be sure that an offence warranting a penalty has been committed, but not certain whether it took place inside the area. For instance, he might have been caught downfield by a long pass and be in no position to judge the exact location of the infringement. Sometimes, it can be down to a matter of inches. This is where the linesman can help. The referee might glance enquiringly at the linesman who, by placing his flag across his chest, can signal that the offence took place in the penalty area.

In my pre-match instructions, I will have already told the linesmen that if a penalty kick is awarded, I want whichever one of them is operating at that end to take up a position somewhere between the goal area intersection with the goal line and the penalty area intersection with the goal line – in otherwords, about ten yards from the post. The linesman's specific and sole task is to determine whether or not the ball crosses the line – and remember the whole of the ball must be over the line. My responsibilities are to supervise and ensure that the kick is taken within the laws.

The first task is to ensure that the kick is actually taken with the ball on the penalty mark and then to identify who is going to take the kick. All players, with the exception of the goalkeeper and the player taking the kick, should be within the field of play, outside the penalty area, and at least ten yards from the ball. In other words, outside the penalty area arc, which is part of the edge of a circle, ten yards in radius and with the penalty mark as its centre.

I will take up a position just outside the goal area and to one side with a good wide-angle view of the goalkeeper, the kicker and the other players. So what am I looking for?

The goalkeeper's feet must be on the line and must remain so until the ball is in play, which is when it has rolled its complete circumference. Often you will hear spectators complaining that the goalkeeper has moved early when, in fact, his feet have remained stationary. He is permitted to move his body and arms. It is his feet that count. If the goalkeeper does move his feet before the ball is in play and he saves the kick, it must be re-taken.

The player who is taking the kick must hit the ball forward and not play it a second time before it touches another player. I remember handling a charity match between Penistone Church and Johnny Quinn's All-Stars a few years ago and during the course of the game, I awarded a penalty kick. The kicker, Quinn himself, played the ball forward for Albert Broadbent to run through and crash the ball into the net. This was the first time I had experienced such a ploy and initially I was a little stunned. 'What do I do now?' I thought. Albert had, in fact, entered the penalty area before the ball had rolled its circumference. So I disallowed the 'goal' and ordered it to be re-taken. From the next kick, a goal resulted, but I was not sure I had made the correct decision and started to sweat a little. I frantically consulted my referees' chart at the earliest opportunity and, to my relief, it transpired that I had done the right thing.

If a defending player encroaches into the penalty area before the ball is in play and the kicker fails to score, the kick would be re-taken and the encroaching player cautioned. Conversely, if an attacking player encroaches and the penalty is successfully converted, it must still be re-taken. The offending player should be cautioned. I recall watching a match between Manchester United and Queen's Park Rangers on television. United were awarded a penalty and, as the kick was being taken, Simon Stainrod, the Rangers forward, pushed a United player in the back and into the penalty area. Stainrod then appealed to the referee that a player had encroached and the kick should be re-taken. The referee must watch for this type of incident. Indeed, there are few areas of the match in which players have not discovered means of employing some form of gamesmanship.

In short, my duty is to ensure the kick is taken within the laws of the game. If a goal is scored, the best thing a referee can do is get the hell out of the area in front of the posts, by running backwards upfield towards the halfway line. He must keep a continual eye on the players, in case there are any flare-ups. A slow walk or jog back to the centre circle often results in a series of disparaging remarks. The defending team will quite likely be unhappy, and there may be a need to issue cautions. A rapid retreat will reduce the chances of having to punish players in this way. Work on the theory that what the ears do not hear, the heart does not feel.

'That was never a penalty' or 'Why didn't the ref give a penalty?' are typical comments when a kick is or is not awarded. Indeed, a penalty is rarely given without prompting some discussion and contrasting opinions. Two penalties I awarded stand out in my mind. One was in the Centenary Cup Final replay – the first penalty awarded in an FA Cup Final for 19 years – and I never had any doubt in my mind that my decision was correct. As Steve Curry, reporting the match for the *Daily Express*, wrote, 'A long free kick by Tommy Caton was headed on to Dave Bennett by Steve Mackenzie. City's striker chested the ball down and, as he turned for goal, went sprawling under the weight of clumsy challenges by Paul Miller and Chris Hughton. It was a clear penalty and Kevin Reeves stepped forward to place his kick positively into the right-hand corner.' Frank McGhee, of the *Daily Mirror*, commented, 'Spurs, if anything, intensified their pressure at the start of the second half, which produced the controversial moment when City went in front. There really should be no controversy. Spurs defender Paul Miller quite clearly shoved City striker David Bennett off the ball illegally inside the area in the fiftieth minute. Kevin Reeves had no trouble at all in scoring from a properly awarded penalty, but for a brief period a great game went sour . . . four cautions in the space of six minutes must create some sort of record.' Indeed, the newspapers were universal in their opinion that I was correct to award a penalty.

But the penalty that remains even more clearly in my mind than that one at Wembley was during a top Second Division match a few years ago between Newcastle United and Wrexham at St James's Park. A Newcastle player, John Brownlie, moving with the ball down the right wing, was fouled but, as he maintained his feet and possession, I signalled and shouted 'play on.' As Brownlie converged on the Wrexham penalty area, Joey Jones, once of Liverpool and now with Huddersfield Town but then playing at full back for Wrexham, grabbed hold of his shirt, pulling him back. Jones managed to kick the ball away, without touching Brownlie's legs, but the shirt-pulling prompted me instantly to award a penalty. The amount of dissent and criticism at my decision from the Wrexham players was enormous.

That evening on *Match of the Day*, whose cameras had been covering the match, both Jimmy Hill and Desmond Lynam strongly criticised my award of the penalty. They used all the evidence at their disposal – slow motions, frozen frames, the works. But they made one crucial mistake. The television concentrated exclusively on the players' feet and Jones taking the ball cleanly. I knew, as much as anybody, that Jones' kicking of the ball away was perfectly legal. But I had not given the penalty for a trip – I had given it for shirt-pulling. Nobody seemed to recognise that.

Most of the television pundits seemed to think I made a mistake by not awarding Tottenham a penalty against Liverpool in the 'live' FA Cup fourth round tie at Anfield in January 1985. I admit that it was a close decision, but I maintain that it was not a penalty. The incident occurred when Ronnie Whelan clipped Tottenham captain Steve Perryman's heel. There is no doubt that contact was made and that it was in the area. My argument is that it was not intentional. Whelan was running back towards his own goal and I believe was scarcely aware of Perryman's presence. Whelan said after the game, 'It was more a case of Perryman's heel hitting my shin. A complete accident, and it would have been harsh if the referee had awarded a penalty.'

Just about everybody else – commentators and newspaper reporters – thought Liverpool were fortunate to escape without conceding a penalty. Brian Moore, Ian St John and Jimmy Greaves were unanimous, but I was only six or seven yards from the incident and the linesman in that half of the field agreed that it was not a penalty. The other linesman, though, thought otherwise.

Liverpool, thanks to a marvellous opportunist goal by Ian Rush, won 1-0 in a match that was in some jeopardy. There had been heavy morning snow and Liverpool secretary Peter Robinson said he wanted a decision by ten to one for a game that started at 2.35 p.m. I attempted to be as positive as possible and asked for the snow to be cleared from around the penalty areas. In the event, with the Anfield undersoil heating working efficiently, the conditions were quite playable.

Another penalty I remember was at Anfield on 27 December 1977. Liverpool were playing Wolves. Maurice Daly, the Wolves midfield player, handled the ball and I awarded a penalty. Phil Neal's first effort was saved by Paul Bradshaw, but there was no doubt in my mind that his feet had moved before the ball was in play and I ordered the kick to be re-taken. As so often in these situations, the defending players argued vehemently and I had to take a couple of Wolves players' names. Anyway, Neal scored with his second attempt and the Liverpool and England full back seemed in no doubt after the game. 'I was conscious that Bradshaw had moved and never had any doubt that I would get another shot. I hit the ball quite hard – and yet he saved it. There's no way he would have got to the ball if he had not moved.'

Penalties, though, do not always go in Liverpool's favour at Anfield. In the 1980 League Cup semi-final, second leg, I awarded a penalty to Nottingham Forest after Ray Clemence had brought down Martin O'Neill. John Robertson scored with the kick. Later in the match, I turned down half a dozen appeals from the Kop for a Liverpool penalty. It is important that referees are not intimidated by the crowd, especially in the crucial area of penalty-giving.

A lot of players cheat in and around the penalty area. A forward who dives when under a perfectly legitimate challenge from a defender in the hope that the referee will award a penalty is cheating. It is natural, perhaps, but it is cheating. Many players have become expert at faking fouls. Let us make no bones about it, a player, when confronted by the goalkeeper or a defender, will often dive. They have developed their skills to such an extent that it is sometimes very difficult to distinguish between a genuine foul and a dive. Some players are clicking their heels, just waiting for the chance to go down. Others, if not awarded the penalty, will look disgusted and robbed of what they try to pretend is their due deserts. It is all designed to put pressure on the referee. Perhaps next time he will give a penalty.

There are several competitions, particularly in Europe, where the result of the match is decided by a penalty 'shoot out' when perhaps a replay and extra time have still failed to produce a winner. The usual format is that each team takes five kicks – or until one gains an unassailable lead – and then, if both have scored an equal number of goals after five kicks, the penalties are taken on a 'sudden-death' basis. It is important that these penalty 'shoot outs' are supervised correctly. Tensions and emotions are usually running high in these situations because the outcome of a match, or even an entire competition, depends on just a few kicks at goal. Few people think the taking of penalties represents an entirely satisfactory way of deciding a match, but, I suppose, it is better than tossing a coin. Try telling that to Graham Rix. He was the man faced with the unenviable prospect of having to score from a penalty kick to prevent Arsenal losing the 1980 European Cup-Winners' Cup Final to Valencia of Spain in Brussels. He missed and collapsed, head in hands, in complete self-reproach. At that moment, few people remembered that Liam Brady's earlier miss had been equally costly to Arsenal.

Most referees, and I am among them, adopt a procedure whereby all the players who are taking the penalty kicks congregate in the centre of the field. One of my linesmen will have a sheet of paper on which is written the name and number of each player. As each player comes forward and shoots at the designated goal – my choice – the linesman can record a kick against the name of that player and whether or not he has scored. The penalty must be taken within the laws but, with all the other players in the middle of the pitch, there is no danger of encroachment. The linesman, though, must still stand in his usual position to check if the ball crosses the line. The referee again watches for early movement of the feet by the goalkeeper and does not award a goal if the 'keeper has moved and the kicker fails to score with his first attempt. As usual, the player cannot score with a second shot from a rebound off the woodwork, but neither, in 'shoot outs' can he score from a rebound off the goalkeeper's body.

Questions and Answers

$$\boxed{13}$$

'What would happen if an earthquake split the pitch in half and the ball fell into the hole?' or 'How would you cope with a manager who drew a gun on you?' or 'Would you punish a player who took his clothes off?' I have been asked all these questions and many, many more. As a referee, people are continually quizzing me about how certain situations should be resolved. Some, like the three mentioned above, bear more relation to fiction than likely reality. Theoretically, they could happen, but it will come as no surprise if I tell you that I have never been confronted by such problems on the football field.

I would like to provide some examples of the type of questions I am often being asked – and the way I answer them. Some of them are, perhaps, slightly hypothetical, but I believe they could occur in a match environment.

Question: What would you do if, during the course of a match, a spectator ran onto the pitch, picked up the ball and ran back into the crowd with it?

Answer: The first thing I would do is blow the whistle. This has the effect of stopping the match and, quite often, seems to stop other people not involved in the game. But I would be careful to try to make as little fuss as possible. For instance, I wouldn't go chasing after the spectator and I wouldn't want any of the players to do so, either. This could incite problems and, especially perhaps if the spectator is a big chap, might result in him suddenly turning round and striking the pursuing player. So I would blow the whistle, attempt to play down the incident as much as possible and re-start the match with a drop ball (a replacement ball if necessary) from the point where the spectator picked it up.

Question: What do you do if a spectator prevents what would otherwise have been a certain goal by encroaching onto the field of play and kicking the ball away?

Answer: Again a drop ball, from the point where the spectator intercepted. It could be that a dog ran onto the pitch. Unlikely, maybe, in the Football League, but possible at a lower level, and there have been occasions when a dog has got onto the pitch during a League game.

Question: Would you allow a match to commence if, when you arrived at the ground, you discovered all the pitch markings were, say, seven inches wide, with the groundsman saying he had done it to allow you, the spectators and players, to see the lines more easily?

Answer: The laws are quite specific on the width of the lines and I would expect them to be no more than the permitted five inches. At the same time, it is unlikely that I would actually get down on my hands and knees and measure the width of the lines with a ruler. It is unlikely to happen in a Football League game. It could occur at a lower level and, in fact, I have seen junior pitches marked with 'tramlines' where the marking machine has not functioned properly and produced a double line. I have had to ask a groundsman to eradicate a line in the past. This can usually be done by scuffing the feet along it or applying extra water and using a brush. At Fulham, for example, where they might have a soccer and rugby league match on successive days, the groundsman uses a green dye to cover up unwanted lines.

Question: What if one of your linesmen were to pull a muscle or injure himself in some way and were unable to continue?

Answer: This could happen to the referee as well as the linesmen. In Football League and FA Cup matches, there is a fourth official standing by and he would come on. If the referee has gone off, the senior linesman would move to the middle. A couple of years ago, I was due to do Queen's Park Rangers against Blackpool in the FA Cup. I was faced with the problem of one of the linesmen not appearing at the ground. An announcement was put out over the tannoy, asking if there were any qualified referees in the ground at Loftus Road. A chap, aged about 47, who had operated on the Isthmian League, answered the call and ran the line in an FA Cup fifth round match. In the event, he performed extremely well. The chances are that, at a big match, there will be somebody suitably qualified. I recall Jimmy Hill once taking the flag when a linesman dropped out at a televised match at Highbury. I believe he did a good job and I'm sure he got first-hand experience of just what running the line in a League match is like.

Question: A team's trainer or physio is not meant to come onto the pitch until signalled to do so by the referee. But what if he does so behind your back and without your approval?

Answer: I would stop the game, approach the scene, gather as much information as possible and then take action. It could be that a player has sustained a very serious injury. A physio, who is the most qualified man within the vicinity of the pitch, might look at a player and see immediately that he is in a bad way and consider that instant attention is required. This has happened to me. I was handling Burnley against Blackpool and a former England youth international called Bobby Tynan, who was playing an early-season Anglo-Scottish Cup game for Blackpool in 1978 (about only his second appearance for the club), went down out of my vision. The game progressed towards the top of the hill at Turf Moor and I turned to see Alan Smith, then the Blackpool physio, bending over the player. Initially, it had not looked particularly serious, because there was nobody around him. But when I ran up to the player it was clear, from the angle of his leg, that he had sustained a very serious injury and that Alan, whom I knew, had done the correct thing by running onto the pitch. He had applied commonsense. Tynan never played again. He suffered damaged knee ligaments and that was the end of his career.

If I thought a trainer had come onto the pitch without my approval purely to waste time, I would take his name and report him to the authorities.

Question: Normally you wait for the ball to go out of play before you beckon the physio onto the pitch. But how about if you saw a player go down, apparently with a serious head wound?

Answer: I would not hesitate to stop the game immediately. I take the view that head injuries can be very serious and there's no way that I will allow the game to continue if I see a player clutching his head and in distress. For instance, Kevin Moran, the Manchester United central defender who seems to get more than his fair share of head injuries, went down with blood spurting from a head wound during the 1983 FA Cup semi-final against Arsenal. In fact, I almost had to catch him. I blew the whistle instantly. I'm not a doctor and I've got people's livelihoods and careers at stake out on the pitch. I don't want to run the risk of somebody becoming serously hurt by delaying his treatment. I would re-start the game with a drop ball.

Question: A player shoots at goal and the ball enters the net. But before the ball does so, it bursts. A goal or not?

Answer: No goal and the game would be re-started by the referee dropping the ball at the place where play was suspended. I understand the ball burst in successive FA Cup Finals shortly after the war. Indeed, the ball went down during the Centenary Cup Final. I think that was caused by stretching. I've never actually handled a game when the ball suddenly punctured, although it is a question that is often asked. It is unfortunate for a player if the ball goes into the net, but the rules state that the ball must be fully inflated . . . the desired weight and the desired circumference.

Question: Can a goalkeeper take a throw-in?

Answer: There's nothing to prevent his doing so.

Question: In rugby, a captain has the power to send off one of his players if he feels he is not trying as hard as he might or for some other reason. Can a soccer skipper do the same?

Answer: No, he can't. The referee is the only person empowered to send off a player. A player can be substituted by the manager or brought off through injury, but not sent off by the captain.

Question: A goal kick goes directly to a forward on the same team, who is standing in an offside position, and he scores. A goal?

Answer: Yes, a goal. Here it is important to highlight the difference between a goal kick and a kick from the goalkeeper's hands. A player cannot be offside from a goal kick, but if he receives the ball from the goalkeeper's hands, then he can be offside. A lot of players – even in the professional game – are not aware of the difference.

Question: How about if the player to whom the goal kick goes touches the ball two or three times to get it under control and, during this time, one of his team-mates runs forward into an offside position?

Answer: It all depends on whether the first player passes the ball. If he does release it to a team-mate, it is offside. But if he maintains possession, then the goal would stand, provided his offside team-mate was not interfering with play at the time.

Question: Corner flags. Could they be two feet high or ten feet high?

Answer: They certainly want to be in the region of five or six feet (not less then five feet is what the laws state). Usually about shoulder high. I was handling a European Cup quarter-final tie at Dinamo Bucharest in March 1984 and commented to the club officials that the corner flags were a little small. They were changed. The reason that they must be five feet or more, of course, is that otherwise there would be a danger that players might fall on top of the flag – potentially very dangerous.

Question: Is a player allowed to remove a corner flag to give himself a decent run at the ball?

Answer: No. The laws are quite specific. Corner flags are compulsory and must remain in their allotted places. Halfway line flags are optional.

Question: Normally, when the ball goes out of play, the referee doesn't stop his watch. But how about if a player, whose team are holding onto a slender lead with just a few minutes remaining, kicks the ball hard and high into touch in a blatant effort to waste time.

Answer: Time-wasting can start right from the kick-off. This is particularly the case in European matches, which are played over two legs. The away team in the first leg are intent on not losing, or at least keeping the margin of their defeat as small as possible, and will do everything to waste the time available for their opponents to shoot at goal. So the referee must be

aware that time-wasting can take place in any game at any stage. It is crucial, therefore, that the referee talks to the players and talks firmly.

He must make the players fully aware of the action that he intends to take. You will sometimes see an exaggerated action from me – holding my wrist, looking at my watch and playing around with the buttons on it. So then everybody has got a pictorial view and will think, 'Yes, the referee is stopping his watch.' The danger for the referee is that the team that is losing could become very frustrated by the action of their opponents and that could lead to violence. If it is a clear, deliberate attempt to waste time, then the referee must caution the player.

Question: How about if you sent off a player and he simply refused to go?

Answer: Then all of us would come off. Fortunately, it has not happened to me. The referee might be able to enlist the services of the captain to persuade the dismissed player to leave the field. In the same way, a captain might be able to confirm the identity of a player who refuses to give his name when cautioned. The referee will have the player's number and can check his name from the teamsheets. In his report he would also mention that this particular player refused to give his name. But if a player refused to leave the pitch, I would pick up the ball and take off all the players. Hopefully, this might persuade the player to go off of his own accord. There was the occasion, of course, in the Sheffield Wednesday v Nigeria friendly when I threatened to enlist the services of a policeman to get a player off. It certainly had the desired effect.

Question: If a player has been substituted and then another player is hit by an object thrown from the crowd, can the original player come back onto the pitch?

Answer: Once a player has been replaced, he cannot return to the action – no matter what the reason. It certainly would be bad luck if a team was reduced to ten men by the intervention of a spectator, but that's all there is to it. It is the same as if a manager has made a substitution and then another of his players is injured. The team is reduced to ten. It is one of the gambles of making a substitution.

Question: A goalkeeper is in possession of the ball in his hands within his own goal area. He passes the ball to a defender who is standing inside his own penalty area. The defender passes it back to the goalkeeper who picks the ball up. Is this okay?

Answer: No. The ball in this instance should have travelled outside the penalty area first. This is an attempt to avoid deliberate time wasting.

Question: A linesman gets into an argument with a player, eventually losing his temper and punching the player unconscious. What action would you take?

Answer: I would send them both off. It is not a totally hypothetical situation, because I have seen officials sometimes lose their rag. I would have to determine exactly what happened – whether the player struck the linesman first, for instance. As a referee, I am at liberty to have the linesman replaced and I would certainly report him to the authorities if he struck a player. Theoretically, I could also have him replaced if I was not satisfied with the standard of his decision-making, but this would surely never happen in a decent league. An official simply wouldn't be carrying a flag if he was not up to scratch. Anyway, even a moderately competent linesman can be utilised to advantage.

Question: A player from the defending team takes a direct free kick and aims it back towards his goalkeeper, who misses it and the ball enters the net. A goal?

Answer: No goal. This is a very common question, but the answer is that a corner kick should be awarded. The same applies if it was an indirect free kick. There was a game between Wimbledon and Millwall at Christmas 1983 when Wimbledon player Wally Downes put a direct free kick into his own goal. Referee John Martin awarded a goal to Millwall, but I'm sure poor old John won't make the same mistake again!